CHERISHED FORTUNE

CHERISHED FORTUNE

Make Your Wealth
Your Business

Andrew Allentuck
and Benoit Poliquin

DUNDURN
TORONTO

Cover image: istock.com/Lesikvit
Printer: Webcom, a division of Marquis Book Printing Inc.

Library and Archives Canada Cataloguing in Publication

Allentuck, Andrew, 1943-, author
     Cherished fortune : make your wealth your business
/ Andrew Allentuck, Benoit Poliquin.

Includes bibliographical references and index.
Issued in print and electronic formats.
ISBN 978-1-4597-4240-6 (softcover).--ISBN 978-1-4597-4241-3
(PDF).--ISBN 978-1-4597-4242-0 (EPUB)

     1. Investments. 2. Portfolio management. I. Poliquin,
Benoit, author II. Title.

HG4521.A44 2018   332.6   C2018-904223-0
                                        C2018-904224-9

1 2 3 4 5   22   21   20   19   18

Conseil des Arts
du Canada
Canada Council
for the Arts
Canada
ONTARIO ARTS COUNCIL
CONSEIL DES ARTS DE L'ONTARIO
an Ontario government agency
un organisme du gouvernement de l'Ontario

We acknowledge the support of the **Canada Council for the Arts**, which last year invested $153 million to bring the arts to Canadians throughout the country, and the **Ontario Arts Council** for our publishing program. We also acknowledge the financial support of the **Government of Ontario**, through the **Ontario Book Publishing Tax Credit** and the **Ontario Media Development Corporation**, and the **Government of Canada**.

Nous remercions le **Conseil des arts du Canada** de son soutien. L'an dernier, le Conseil a investi 153 millions de dollars pour mettre de l'art dans la vie des Canadiennes et des Canadiens de tout le pays.

Care has been taken to trace the ownership of copyright material used in this book. The author and the publisher welcome any information enabling them to rectify any references or credits in subsequent editions.
                                        — J. Kirk Howard, President

The publisher is not responsible for websites or their content unless they are owned by the publisher.

Printed and bound in Canada.

VISIT US AT

dundurn.com | @dundurnpress | dundurnpress | dundurnpress

Dundurn
3 Church Street, Suite 500
Toronto, Ontario, Canada
M5E 1M2

TABLE OF CONTENTS

PREFACE

We have written *Cherished Fortune: Make Your Wealth Your Business* in the belief that most instructional books on investment needlessly complicate the process. From the inspirational work *The Wealthy Barber* to the seminal works in financial analysis starting with Graham and Dodd's *Security Analysis*, the process has been variously turned into a form of self-belief, which is the common currency of inspirational investment books, and in varying levels of complexity, manuals on computation. Most of these works view investing in financial assets and real estate as an abstraction distant from daily life. Some of the work published in academic journals needs the skills of a mathematician to decipher. Directness and clarity have been lost.

We take a different view, that buying stocks and bonds, real estate, and other at-risk assets is not so different from what a person does running his or her own small business. It is a matter of understanding what you have to offer, the assets and knowledge, the cost of inventory for sale, the liabilities, the money coming in and going out — that is, the income statement — and the tax implications of the business done. From this perspective, a portfolio of assets is a small business that one can run with intimate knowledge of its parts. It's like a corner store, if you accept the analogy.

The idea that investment analysis must be a cat's cradle of numerical analysis has developed from professions that profit from complexity. For regulatory reasons and from the wish to satisfy accounting standards, the quarterly and annual reports of public companies run to scores or hundreds of pages of income composition, changes in assets and liabilities, legal risk, accounting system reconciliation, and footnotes to support all of this. Each division of a large company reports in much the same depth. The disclosures satisfy regulations, but whether they add to understanding or even can be understood is quite another matter.

We approach this complexity with both comprehension of what the numbers are about, for Andrew Allentuck is by training an economist with decades of experience reading and writing long equations, and Benoit Poliquin is a chartered financial analyst who reads and writes the language of accounting with its long tails of numbers and investigations into income statements and balance sheets of potential investments.

We think that the basic question for any investor who proposes to invest in the shares of a company they do not run and cannot control, and for which their only power is that to elect directors, is intellectual. Specifically, the would-be investor should ask the most basic question of all: How do these guys make their money? That is the foundation of investment analysis, and it is also the most sensible first question. The problem of understanding is fundamental, for when you buy into somebody else's business by taking on either its debt via a bond or its ownership via stock, or even by buying a parcel of land with or without a building on it, the seller knows a lot more about the asset than you do. The situation has a name, information asymmetry, and the solutions are variously in the realms of accounting and fancy equations — or, what we prefer, direct and simple common sense. We want to get past the myths and down to the works of the assets one wishes to buy or, if profits are realized or losses threaten or may worsen, to sell.

It leads to looking at sales and costs, then to the difference, which is profit. Where there are long times between investment and realization of income — for example, in such capital-intensive industries as making electric power or connecting telephones through costly networks — return on money invested in the business is critical. Competition comes into all this, of course, for if another company has a better mousetrap, the firm in question's sales may be compromised.

The paradigm of *Cherished Fortune* is to invest as you would in your own small business, with a tactile feel for every asset. Know what you have, and expand your portfolio as your knowledge of markets and assets grows. Do not abdicate to others or to concepts like the dot-coms or, more recently, the BRICs (Brazil, Russia, India, China), which have of late turned into a flopped concept, for Brazil is in financial disarray and Russia's economy is a mess of rising mortality and dependence on the price of hydrocarbon exports. The essence of the book is to advance the idea of investing with what you know, not what others say. It is a simple idea, yet rarely advocated and less often followed. We have organized *Cherished Fortune* by process of investing into the areas of most interest to folks who invest, and in doing so we have examined motives for investment and assets traded.

We look at the motivations of crowds, which, though they may be the swirling masses throwing their money into things they do not understand, nevertheless furnish the liquidity all markets need. Crowds, right or wrong, are the foot soldiers of trends. They cannot be ignored. Markets cannot exist without many players, yet mob think and the tendency of outsiders to rush in heedless of the risks to their fortunes can push up asset prices to unsustainable levels. We examine the mechanics and offer some antidotes.

Debt is the leverage of real estate and of all businesses that use others' capital to make money. Debt can be productive, in that it can be used to buy assets, or it can be anticipatory, used for consumption. Leverage can add return, but it also adds risk. It is general, it is part of what many companies do to increase their muscle in the market, and it adds risk to their businesses. Well used, debt makes businesses bigger and stronger. Ill used, it weakens them.

Valuation is the question of what something is worth. It should be part of any investment decision. Accountants have a word — goodwill — to explain why some people pay more than a thing is worth in terms of its plant and equipment. It can explain the premium a good business commands, or it may be a hole into which good money is thrown, never to be seen again.

Bonds are the most traditional way business has been financed. Debt documents are found in the records of ancient Babylon, and for millennia enterprise was financed by borrowing rather than by sharing ownership. In our tax system, interest on debt is deducted from operating income, unlike dividends of businesses, which are a way of sharing profit with owners. The balance is what makes or breaks an investment. We give that balance careful examination, as would any shop owner wondering whether to borrow to expand the business, to sell a piece of it to a friend or neighbour, or to even get together with a competitor to gain market strength.

Stocks are ownership, complex in their operation, simple in the idea of being a way for outsiders to share in the fortunes of the business selling the shares. We strip away the complexity to find ways to discern which stocks are promising and which are toxic to one's fortune. We look at how returns are measured, the long-run return data and risk management by value metrics, the sustainability of trends, and selection methods, risk, and price variability.

Real estate, it is said, is a rare resource and usually rises in price. Neither is true. Office buildings are constructed on air rights, cities expand into cornfields and even over water, and abandoned buildings can be gentrified into fashionable and expensive living space. The property market is typically illiquid, for it takes much wheedling and lawyering to transact a land deal. But land and buildings are tangible. You can touch them, unlike stocks and bonds that are no longer even traded on paper. They are claims documented as ledger entries. It is no wonder that land and buildings fascinate investors — with a visit, you can see what you own. We discuss leverage and the question of who carries interest rate risk, equity risk and the idea that the home depreciates while the underlying land appreciates, what part of a home is an equity investment and what part is just rent for occupancy, the special tax characteristics of homes, and return on equity on the home as investment and the home as shelter providing occupancy services.

Mistakes are inevitable and seldom given their due. One can learn from them and sometimes correct them. We examine the anatomy of error to find ways to fix them and ways to avoid them by discussing the problem of knowing what you don't know, our thoughts on why skepticism in numerical form is an investor's life preserver, and tests that can identify the foolishness of crowds. Even more instructive than success, error, when understood, shows the path to enhanced future performance.

The investor's protections against market misfortunes are management of liquidity risk and diversification. History proves that these defences are vital, since investing in others' work is inevitably precarious. Our concluding chapter shows that investment analysis is far from being the esoteric work of specialists, a great many of whom do worse than throwing darts at targets marked "buy" or "don't buy," "sell" or "hold," relying on their own myths of knowledge. Few consistently beat random answers half right and half wrong. An investor who knows their own risks and wallet, their purpose and plan, can do better. Making that happen is the goal of *Cherished Fortune*.

Cherished Fortune is a metaphor: that is, the idea that you can enter financial management using the concept of a small business as a model for your portfolio. You can learn the business from the ground up, understanding what works, what does not, and controlling risk by increasing your knowledge of assets and their management. It is the idea of intimacy with what is in the portfolio, learning how each stock and the company behind it works. It is the approach of the great investor, Warren Buffett, head of Berkshire-Hathaway, but on a smaller and more intimate scale. Our approach is learning intelligent asset management from the ground up in terms anyone can understand. In this business, knowledge of what you are doing beats faith in others. That is the goal of the book and that is what we have set out to show.

INTRODUCTION

The Sense of Investing in Others' Businesses

How do successful investors get to be that way? The steps they take to increase their wealth make up a taxonomy of talents and goals. So much of the literature on how to make money in stocks and bonds, real estate, antiques, art, autographs, and more is about details and histories of prices of this and that. It is looking backward to go forward, which is a dangerous practice if you are driving.

We have a much simpler idea: Run your portfolio as though it were small business you know well. Even though you are buying into others' businesses, ask this fundamental question any time you give somebody your money: What makes the business function as a tradeoff of people giving it their money for whatever the business will return as income or capital gains?

In the complicated books on stock and bond analysis, little discussion is directed to answer that basic question. Why throw money into somebody else's business? If you understand the business well enough to answer the question — how does this thing work? — you are off to a good start.

In the bulletins stock brokers send to their clients and in press stories of how businesses are faring, much attention is given to earnings formulations and price-to-sales ratios. In bonds the focus is on macroeconomics and credit ratings. In commercial real estate, it is on ratios of rent to cost. All that matters, of course. But the main thing that you need to be able to answer is that question of what makes the profits. From the top line of how much money they ring in as sales to the bottom line of what is left for the owners — that is, those who hold the common stock — you need to be able that question: How does it work? Next question: If I throw my money into their pot, what do I get? What's in it for me?

These are basic and essential questions, yet the answers are often made complex by fancy numerical analysis done by men and women with fine academic diplomas and lavish resumés attesting to their acumen. The unspoken secret of the academic/professional analyst biz is that they stick together. And when these well-bred and well-educated analysts work for investment banks, they know that saying unkind things about client companies is not going to advance their careers. Thus, the vast majority of analysts' reports from the so-called sell side of the investment business are positive. For the would-be private investor, a dose of cynicism is in order.

Our plan, and this book's plan, is to cut through the complexity of conventional financial analysis and its invocations of mathematical formulas and statistics to what amounts to common sense. We'll show that paying too much for assets that are always under conditions of uncertainty — after all, nobody knows what trouble a company can get into — is unnecessary. Many of the analysts who hype stocks that are unreasonably expensive work for investment banks that sell the very same shares. There is safety in calculating your own figures.

We should tip our hats to the literature that defines success and traces the steps to it. Financial magazines are often awash with stories of billionaires, their original Renoirs, and their yachts. There is nothing new in this form of envy. It is Biblical, in that it's critical in making the distinction between the realms of God and of Caesar. It is literary, appearing from Greek drama to the modern stage — think of Oscar Wilde's *The Importance of Being Earnest* and the pathology of failure captured in Arthur Miller's *Death of a Salesman* — and in the current fascination with the careers of Steve Jobs, Warren Buffett, Bill Gates, and other capitalists whose businesses have thrived on what could be called a single idea. The problem with the latter literature is that it represents the successful explaining how they got to be that way. It is backward looking. Each tycoon's story is distinct and not necessarily repeatable. In any event, you can't start out being General Motors.

We propose that growing one's wealth by investing in others' businesses by buying stocks and bonds and by buying real estate for development or rental can be done with manageable risk and good prospects for gains. The more you know about your market — in other words, your portfolio, your costs, the achievability of profit targets, and the risks you face — the better your prospects for gain.

Many people, seeing the vast number of choices of stocks and bonds, real estate projects, and even collectibles, give up. We think that's wrong. You cannot understand the world of finance the first time you see it, but you can grow into it, much as you might open a small store and see its sales and profits grow and turn eventually into a larger business with diverse lines of activity. You cannot have it all at once, but you can learn the ropes and climb them.

> You cannot understand the world of finance the first time you see it, but you can learn the ropes and climb them.

TIME AND REALIZATION

How do you judge the success or failure of an investment? A stock may fall after purchase only to rise to astounding heights a few months or years afterward. The investor who expects instant gratification is likely to be disappointed. Even Amazon.com took four years from 2013 to rise from US$275 to the recent price of about US$1,626. If you want faster outcomes, you should go to a casino. Stocks and bonds and real estate seldom have the swift resolution of gambling tables.

Cynics say that buying stocks on tips or even on trends, which are collective tips of winners asking others to join them, is a form of industrial gambling. We concur. The difference between this kind of gambling, which is little more than a play on price, and informed investing is understanding the stocks' business much as you would understand your own business, and earning dependable income flows that can pay you back even if the stock tumbles and stays down. All this may seem boring, but it is caution put into practice. Be humble about what you know, for in most cases, you will know less than what you do not know. This is humility. It is also honest.

The advice that teaches success tends to be variously inspirational and technical. There are attitudinal books, many rooted in the 1970s, when reforming the self was seen as vital in such neo-theological themes as Rolfing, Esalen, and the cults of various swamis and gurus, not to mention the tongue-in-cheek distillations of business wisdom from the writing and attributed sayings and doings of Genghis Khan ("Don't negotiate, conquer"), Machiavelli ("It is better to be feared than loved, if you cannot do both"), Abe Lincoln ("Better to be silent and thought a fool than to speak and remove all doubt"), and so on.

We take the view that fundamental human traits measured by commitment, patience, focus, and a deep understanding of one's endeavours can enlarge one's fortune.

This is transitory wisdom — clever, but not necessarily applicable to managing money. As well, there are skill-based advisory books that seek to transfer wisdom and investing technique from applications in such things as engineering.

We take the view that fundamental human traits measured by commitment, patience, focus, and a deep understanding of one's endeavours, which are the foundations of successful lives, can enlarge one's fortune. The top-line concept is that investors should stay within their circles of competence. Don't buy what you do not understand, and certainly not because a friend or relative is buying it. Swift jabs into things of which one knows little, such as investments in flavour-of-the-moment companies on the web, are likely to fail. It is the greater fool theory gone digital. Then, however, as one's knowledge and expertise, experience, and acquired sense of self-preservation grow, one can invest further afield. None of this should seem startling. What is shocking, on the other hand, is how swiftly novice investors pile into bad ideas.

There is a simple numerical test for how well ideas pay. In stocks, the ratio of price per share to earnings per share (the p/e ratio) is a key guide to value. Canadian chartered banks typically have p/e ratios of twelve. That means a dozen years of future earnings will repay your investment in that time or less if you add in the dividends. Some hot web stocks have p/e ratios of two hundred or more. You will have to wait two centuries for the return of your money if there is no dividend, and there usually isn't. Even if earnings double, you will have to wait a century. If earnings quadruple, you'll need to wait a more modest fifty years. Investors in these hot stocks are not betting on earnings trends. They are betting on the enthusiasm of other investors. We think that's industrial gambling, not so far from shooting craps in Vegas.

Investors in dot-coms in the last years of the twentieth century threw money at companies labelled "digital" that had no sales, no profits, no business plans, and no experience in markets and that, to top it all off, were prized for burning up other people's money. No corner grocer would invest in goods their customers do not want. Paradoxically, in the investment world, unfamiliarity with assets seems no barrier to casting money to the winds. Compared to a casino, stock market bubbles large — the ones we know — and small — they happen every day — are like games the players do not know how to play with odds they cannot fathom. This is idiotic. We think the small shopkeeper knows their own business best. The task of this book is to help transfer that innate, experienced-based knowledge to the larger and more complex world of investing in capital markets.

CENTS AND SENSIBILITY

Good sense is often missing in capital markets, especially at a time when markets are in a rising bull phase. The warning signs of overconfidence show up when investment ideas are packaged for sale rather than for long-run success. Florida land, New York skyscrapers in the 1920s, and miracle diets are old hat. Many new ideas are born from false correlations. The number of people in the U.S. killed each year by venomous spiders may fluctuate at the same rate as the number of marriages each year in Kentucky, but close as the correlations may be, they are false, for it is unlikely that one trend has anything to do with the other. In securities markets, there are approximately 100,000 index numbers published each day, from the Dow Jones Industrial Average to the hides and tallow index. That some of these will be correlated, and that some will seem to be leading predictors of others, is certain. Milton Friedman, the late and great American monetary economist, suggested that if a correlation works, go with it.[1] Rejecting an association could mean one would not learn a new relationship. That is a valuable tip for academic research. But for the modest task of making money, we say that if it makes no sense, don't go with it.

A MATTER OF RISK

We need to talk about risk and time. One can, with luck, achieve a great fortune in Las Vegas or in capital markets by taking on a great deal of short-term risk. A few dollars can generate a million in a few slot machines, but it doesn't happen very often. Those who sit and play for a long time are more likely to lose to the house advantage. Indeed, that is almost certain, for the casinos could not operate without capturing more going into their games than going out.

There is no house advantage, per se, in capital markets, where one trades most of the time with other investors, but it is not a zero-sum game either, in which all gains equal all losses. The costs of trading, even if small, accumulate. Dealers grow rich even if their clients lose their shirts. Moreover, some of the other investors are huge hedge funds, trading desks of brokerages, and computers trading vast sums in microseconds. However, the cost of error, whether in assessment of risk or of value, means that there is no equivalence between winners and losers. Those who gamble in these markets, assuming that the odds are with them through shrewd buys and sells, have to deduct the cost of error from their potential wins. The odds are that speculators will suffer large losses from time to time. The winners will be those investors who grow their fortunes carefully, amassing knowledge and a feel for their markets and assets. They gain advantages this way that outsiders cannot have.

As the time for play or commitment to an enterprise grows, human values gain importance. It is in this space of years and decades that patience, frugality, concentration, tending to customers, and understanding and developing employees come into their own. Look at the careers and achievements of those who built empires, and, with few exceptions, they share common traits of giving a great deal of thought to their work, understanding what people want, knowing what their technologies can do, balancing present cost with future gain, and, above all, of sticking to what they know and learning more about what they do as they do it.

There is also the matter of knowing when to quit. The names of those who did not and of businesses that sputtered when they did not move with the times are familiar. Think of Polaroid Corp., which stuck with a chemical photo process at the dawn of digital photography; ditto Kodak, which was late to the digital imaging business; ITT, short for International Telephone & Telegraph, a conglomerate of meaningless components that sputtered and came apart; and computer makers from Commodore International to Atari, DEC, and many more, which, though once sensible, lost sense as markets separated achievers from plodders.

> There is no house advantage in capital markets, but it is not a zero-sum game either, in which all gains equal all losses.

Polaroid and Kodak had sunset technologies. The problem with these investments is that, through their time as glamour stocks, which for each lasted many years, the investor had to recognize the folly of investing in a dying industry. Yet on the way down, companies can be tempting to investors, because the ratio of price to earnings will decline and, with lower stock prices, the ratio of dividend to price, the yield, will rise. Some companies may even give back a lot of capital through share buybacks, in the recognition that they cannot employ it well. Investing in a death spiral is squandering capital. Only good sense and understanding the business can prevent an investor following quantitative guidelines from throwing their money away.

WHAT IDEAS ARE PORTABLE?

Is success transferrable from one job or application to another, or is it embedded in a place of employment or, for that matter, a certain type of asset that has done well? In other words, how specific are the skills that lead to success? Can an engineer become a great investor? Of course. A chemist a great capitalist? Certainly — biotech companies often have fabulous returns on their equity and profits on sales. But there is a hidden secret in this business: Much of the capital is not readily counted. It is in the minds and training of the scientists who work on making new drugs. If their cost of education and the value of what they do were put into the denominator of returns, the ratios would be much lower. The scientists transfer their knowledge to products for sale, and many of the products are fabulously profitable. But these transfers are one-way, because a record of success on Bay Street or Wall Street will not get one a teaching post in the sciences at any good university.

And yet, the idea that a gifted employee can take his or her accomplishments from one area or occupation — whether it be medicine, engineering, geology, or French literature — and transfer the skills that engendered academic success to another endeavour is speculative. Insights into new technologies lie behind the meteoric rise of Apple Inc., Microsoft Corp., and, of course, that temple to friendship, Facebook. We'll return to this phenomenon of transference of skills to capital markets. It is the essence of our theory of investing: doing what you know and expanding from that island of information to the nations and continents of capital. We would add that Apple's Steve Jobs, Microsoft's Bill Gates, and Facebook's Mark Zuckerberg all stuck to what they knew. Focus built their fortunes. They did not build empires by shotgun investing. Each focused on the business he knew and built, at least until it got to be so large that others had to handle the massive profits.

It's old-fashioned to suggest this, but always start with what you know. The alternative is to buy because others are buying lest one miss out. It remains a curiosity that investors, who are supposedly a thoughtful lot who have been able to save a surplus for putting into other people's businesses, can be swept up in waves of enthusiasm. The roster of failed concepts runs from those Dutch tulips in the seventeenth century to Florida land speculation to lists of stocks everyone should have, such as the Nifty Fifty of the 1960s — a list of flops whose growth subsided into stagnation, although a few, including Walmart, did very well. In every one of these cases, investors plunged into a theory they did not understand and abandoned great investments, such as Canadian chartered bank shares, which languished in the dot-com mania of the late 1990s, when they were sold to provide money for the weird and wonderful things on the web.

Investing in ignorance was really what was happening. The consequence of this process is clear. Without knowing the merits of an asset, its future earnings, or its value on the balance sheet, it's like going to a buffet blindfolded. There's no telling what you may get, and the combination may be unpalatable.

> It remains a curiosity that investors, supposedly a thoughtful lot, can be swept up in waves of enthusiasm.

Given the demonstrated failure of investing in the unknown, one is entitled to ask: What is the nature of the intelligence that allows one to find fortune in others' businesses? What are the catalysts, which are luck or chance, and which are irrelevant? W.S. Gilbert, librettist for Sir Arthur Sullivan, raises this issue in *HMS Pinafore*. The Admiral of the Queen's Navy rises to his position on numerous skills, including penmanship. None of these skills, however, has anything to do with the sea. The reverse concept is the Peter Principle, which holds that people rise to their level of incompetence. The humour of both parodies is in the idea that success goes to the incompetent. In a statistical sense, however, one suspects that the combinations of intellect, personality, being in the right place at the right time, making a timely trade in capital markets by chance, and perhaps being in touch with the indicia of timing that the others respect — for example, so-called technical analysis (following asset prices on the theory that past wobbles predict future ones) — will produce divergent results. This is a rule of outliers. One can massage the data to produce a correlation, a best-fit line that brings it all together, but when deviance from averages rules, whatever rules are found are suspect.

THE VALUE OF ACQUIRED KNOWLEDGE

In *Cherished Fortune*, we take the view that it is essential to invest outside of one's work if only to diversify risk, but that every investment must be well understood before it is made. This is not to say that there is no external risk that can harm or destroy one's plans. Even the best-laid plans are vulnerable — factories to rare floods, businesses to technological change, careers to illness, and life itself to stepping off the curb at the moment a truck rumbles by.

> It is essential to invest outside of one's work if only to diversify risk, but every investment must be well understood before it is made.

Our view, however, is that one should mitigate risk by investing close to home at first in things one knows or senses. Thus anyone in Canada who reads the newspaper or watches television news has some sense of what the chartered banks are doing, how fuel costs affect airlines, and what is happening to energy and mining. This is a valuable edge in capital markets. An investor working from the sidelines and told that the price of Air Canada or a chartered bank is soon to double can ask the appropriately cynical question — "Why should it?" — and then take a measure of the answer. Stocks do double, some unexpectedly. The investor in Canada is able to sense what is true or false in market prophecies. Our model Canadian investor is probably less able to describe what a British bank, say National Westminster, is up to and how it is faring, or how publicly traded Swiss drug makers, Indian steel makers, Chinese telecoms, and South African mines are doing. Familiarity is a huge asset in trusting others with one's savings.

The advantage of being in a market and having a feeling for it is at least as valuable as the edge a Canadian or North American investor may gain from reading about esoterica like the recently hot Mongolian rare earth biz. That's the stuff that goes into a lot of electronic circuits. Chromium, lithium, and other rare metals have the unfortunate habit of existing in faraway places. An outsider, which is to say anyone not versed in making electronics parts and mining what goes into them, is dabbling in this field even with the guidance of brokerage research reports. It is precarious. You might hear that some company digging ores that make metals used in cell phones will have its share price double. You can accept that or not. If you hear that the Royal Bank is about to double its revenues or profits, your sense of balance will urge you to ask why it should.

It is a paradox of capital markets that learned men and women, experts in their own fields, will throw money to the winds when tempted by a seemingly sensible theory. Modern portfolio theory has proven that the sum of many high risks, say twenty stock indices in twenty different countries, twenty assets in all, each with a 50/50 chance of falling, will have a 60 percent chance of gain. The argument is that each marches to a different drummer and that, with a process of selling one index when it is up a given amount, say 10 percent, and using the profit to buy another when it is down 10 percent, the whole affair will inevitably grow. Yes, in theory, but like the older idea that return rises with risk, it only works over the long run. But no one really knows what the long run is. It has neither clock nor calendar. It could be next year or the next century. Lives are finite and our needs are definite. Statistical analysis and theories will work in the long term, yet most of us will operate in the span of a few decades, not centuries. This is not a trivial observation. The long run in a personal sense is no more than our actual lives or life expectancies. That is the maximum period of proof for any idea. That sets the most meaningful goal posts for our ideas to work or fail.

We would rather invest in a model defined as concentric circles, starting in one's own career, paying off student loans, then perhaps in a home, paying off a mortgage, then in a family, and all the while adding surplus money to investments chosen by familiarity. Thus one could buy Canadian banks and telecoms and be protected in part by their dividends, which, over time, can pay for a lot of stock price declines, then buy manufacturing companies that have neither the massive oligopoly status of banks nor the massive capital requirements of telecommunications companies nor the protections of regulators looking after power utilities. Note that banks do stumble and a few collapse — think of Lehman Brothers' crushing collapse in 2008 and, in the same year, the sale of investment bank Bear Stearns for just US$10 a share to JPMorgan Chase, or, closer to home, the Canadian Commercial Bank, then the largest bank insolvency in Canadian history, which flopped in 1985 after a brief lifespan of nine years, followed later in 1985 by the flop of the Northland Bank. The Canadian cases were flops of management. Those collapses show that even safe bets can and often do crumble. And no bank is immune from sudden interest rate changes that make some loans unprofitable nor from economic cycles, such as the collapse of global oil prices, which make other loans uncollectible. The point: Read the papers and be informed, but always be a cynic. Do not invest beyond your knowledge. That means No! to tips, regardless of the source.

CAPITAL EMIGRATION: DIVERSIFICATION WITH REASON

With experience and rising fortune, one can invest farther from home. Canadian investors can move some money to American megafirms like Johnson & Johnson or European brands like L'Oreal or Diageo. Their products are everywhere and yet their results are rarely on the front page of any financial press. You can, however, take a stroll to your nearest restaurant or drug store and understand why they are a financial success.

Peter Lynch, a famous portfolio manager who ran the Fidelity Magellan fund, one of the most successful mutual funds ever to operate in the United States, urged buying observable assets; that is, those that can be seen in a shopping mall of retailers or a car lot, drug store, or grocery store. Between 1977 and 1990 Magellan averaged an annual return of over 29 percent, making Magellan the best performing mutual fund in the world.[2] His concept was called "buy what you know." It is a viable idea, but financial knowledge is not intuitive. There is no substitute for study and observation. The counterpart is that there is no cushion for losses that come from not knowing the risks in any investment.

As one goes farther afield, insights become vague and it is harder to follow trends. The devices for diversification, such as low-fee exchange traded funds (ETFs), make it possible to buy into a country or an industry. Diversification reduces single company risk. The ETF's structure, fees, and history are readily available. If a region is going into some sort of recovery, one can buy an ETF that replicates its components by component weight; for example, a Far East ETF with or without Japan or a Chinese industry ETF.

In this learning process, the components of the portfolio should be heavily weighted with what you know best and lightly weighted with what you know least. Having money on the table is an incentive to learn and follow.

A critic of this investment concept can say it's just mirrors. The idea of diversification is to get far from home and domestic risk, far from one's job and its risks. We have no argument with this, but our view is tempered and patient. Buy into what you understand and learn more. True, at first you may have a view that is more mirror than picture window, but the transition of views will come. Safety, we believe, is in the investor's most important asset. That asset is not what is in his or her wallet, but what is in his or her head.

> Financial knowledge is not intuitive — there is no substitute for study and observation.

Paradoxically, investors have given up much of the job of managing their wealth to the funds management industry. The theory of diversification, that one can gain by moving money far afield and into other countries and assets, a sort of premium return for unfamiliarity, ignores the difficulties of timing entrances in and out of volatile economies, such as those of emerging markets, and asset classes that are golden one day and dross the next. Moreover, many national indices, especially in the developing world, are not investable. One cannot buy into an index that replicates some of these small markets, particularly in Africa below the Sahara. In the end, the math presumes rewards for what amounts to an academic exercise in structured faith, or faith in a theory, or blind ignorance — take your pick. This kind of investing by faith in something or someone else or some theory poorly understood has enough defects to doom unlucky investors who do not know and often do not care what others have picked for them.

One may save for decades and then entrust savings to a manager with a theory and a business card, then seldom look back. The irony is inescapable: it is ironic that investors hire professionals to invest on their behalf and abdicate asking questions. It should be said that money managers have done well with this disconnect. As *The Economist* noted in a March 5, 2016, survey of fund management entitled "Living Off the People," a quarter of all American billionaires work in finance and investments, an industry that employs just 1 percent of the population.[3] It is essential to hire right and then be vigilant. So, first, make sure the manager is a seasoned professional; second, make the manager accountable; and third, understand how the manager is compensated.

THE TRANSFER PROBLEM: IS INVESTING A LESS THAN ZERO-SUM GAME?

In economics, the distinction between the long run and the short run is undefined. Everything is supposed to work out or become visible in the long run, whatever that is. Short could mean the next minute in some very fast stock market trades, and long could mean thirty-year credit cycles in the bond market where some cycles are measured in centuries.[4] No one can distinguish long from short except by assumption or in retrospect, but the distinction is crucial in answering this question: Does it pay to buy stocks and bonds and all the other stuff like options, which are rights to buy or sell, or futures, which are forward purchases of things, often agricultural?

In the short run, much investing is just taking from Peter to pay Paul, a theological idea that has been traced back to the fourteenth-century English theologian John Wycliffe, who could be considered to have asked what value there is in obedience to dysfunctional ideas. A heretic in his time, whose bones were burned after his body was exhumed after burial, he put the problem of transfer squarely in view. If you get nothing for something, why do it?[5]

This is the conundrum of investing. At any moment on a stock market, one person sells, another buys. It's not an even trade, for there will be transfer costs such as commissions large or slight; tax, perhaps, to be paid; and uncertainty as to whether the trade was good for one, for both, or for neither if the stock falls and the seller buys something else that also falls. Yet over the long run, if costs of trading and management can be kept in check, all parties in the market can and will benefit. How can this be if, in the short run, both may lose?

The answer has several parts. First, for those who stay invested in stocks and bonds — anything with a better future than cash or gold — inflation alone will boost stock asset value and, over time, bonds will have a return based on interest, which, one may say, is the auction price of money including anticipation of inflation. Interest rates during the recovery from the meltdown of 2008 to 2009 were less than the rate of inflation; that is, negative in real terms.

Stock prices rise in part because the post-inflation cost of money for corporate investment has been low. This is the real transfer of value from Peter to Paul. And if we say that Peter is the holder of bonds lending money at less than the cost of inflation to stockholder Paul, the cost of the transfer is negative. Paul gains. Peter loses.

> The goal is to reduce randomness and increase the probability of winning, and to do this in expanding circles of knowledge and opportunity.

The goal is to reduce randomness and increase the probability of winning, and to do this in expanding circles of knowledge and opportunity. That process results in better decisions. In effect, you want to increase your chances of a successful outcome and/or reduce the impact of mistakes, much like a hitter in baseball or a golfer. The home runs and long drives get you into the limelight, but the lack of mistakes gets you the success and big contracts.

THE THEORY AND THE REALITY OF RISK MANAGEMENT

This is not so radical an idea. Modern portfolio theory demonstrates that one can do very well with reduced risk and increased returns by spreading one's money over many companies, industries, and markets. This is true. But it does not work if the spread or the ratio is wrong. If you want to use the theory, then buy half a dozen global funds, each with differing ratios of market weights — more U.S. or less E.U., currency hedged or not, with or without Japan, heavier or lighter on

China. If you buy just one global market ETF, you could have the one with the wrong ratios. As Peter Lynch, the famed driver of mutual funds for Fidelity in Boston, said, "If you buy into an industry or into an idea, buy at least three stocks with it. If you buy just one, it's going to be the wrong one."

Selection turns out to be the Achilles heel of diversification. Rather than suffer from it, we believe that by starting with what you know, you can broaden your portfolio, working toward the core idea of the theory of diversification. But before the novice investor starts diversifying, he or she should stick to home. If your wealth is your business, stay with what you know.

By starting with what you know, you can broaden your portfolio, working toward the core idea of the theory of diversification.

A word on diversification is in order. Diversification's optimal product is called the "efficient frontier." It is the mathematical expression of getting the best possible and probable yield from combining many assets into one portfolio with a given level of risk. It is a form of fancy math. But don't be fooled. This is great stuff for courses in mathematical finance at top-flight universities with crummy football teams, but it is not a way to get the cash to accelerate your mortgage payments.

A math concept will illustrate the basis for a sound portfolio construction. If one buys five stocks and weights them equally, each stock will have a 20 percent importance. If one of these goes to zero, the investor is out 20 percent. That will be a tough road to recovery.

Alternatively, if one buys thirty or forty stocks and weights them equally, each stock will have a degree of importance of about 2.5 percent to 3.33 percent. If a stock were to go to zero, the loss would be much more manageable. You might say that it works the other way, too, cutting the gains from a few winners. But inflation and usually competent management tend to raise corporate earnings. If you invest in big, well-known companies that pay dividends, the odds of gain are on your side.

There are limits to diversification, for many exchange traded funds that imitate various market indices have hundreds of stocks in them.

That reduces the chance that any single company can wreck your portfolio, but this dilution means that you cannot track each company very well. Keeping track of a dozen or two names is one thing, but following two hundred names is beyond the ability of most folks. Too many bets with too many moving parts is a self-defeating strategy.

You could put the contrast between the idea of the efficient frontier, which allows blind investing in indices on the theory that they do not dance to the same beat at the same time, with the core idea of fundamental investing — know thy asset. Our judgment: The idea of the efficient frontier, and all the mathematics wrapped up in the notion of an efficient frontier, requires so much diversification and so much monitoring to keep ratios of this national index and that asset class in line that it is less workable for the small investor than buying what is locally known, familiar, and able to be analyzed with a careful review of its financial statements.

If we seem to be advocating an anachronism, well, we are. Our view is that every investor has innate knowledge that can be put to good use, especially if enhanced with some book work such as reading the financial press, studying finance, and reviewing high school algebra. This approach, which could colloquially be called "back at ya," is a strong suggestion that the investor will do well to trust his or her own counsel. Not necessarily to the fine points of judging the condition of a bank's balance sheet or the risks embedded in its loans, but to the wider and more general concept of what the portfolio is for and how to get from the balance sheet to one's own stock's profits.

CALLS FOR HELP

As the writer of the *Financial Post*'s Family Finance series and as president and lead portfolio manager of Exponent Investment Management, Allentuck and Poliquin, respectively, hear from people desperate to know why their investments have fared badly. Their hopes crushed by bad luck or bad management, for these people the outcomes are inevitably unacceptable losses. And almost as inevitably, it is the result of high fees paid by people who trust the ladies and gentlemen tasked by their banks or other employers to sell, sell, and sell more. Occasionally there are port-folios of weirdly wrong asset combinations, such as inverse plays on complex options that go up in value when underlying assets go down. In every case, the aggrieved or bewildered investor could have asked the advisor at the bank or brokerage or fund-selling firm the critical question: What is this or that fund or stock supposed to do for me? How does it work? Those questions could have saved fortunes.

The investor, even a neophyte properly worried about loss, must ask what the advisor hopes to deliver for the money.

There is a bad match between financial advisors who have easily acquired letters after their names and clients who are much too impressed with the letters. The old saying "Don't ask a barber if you need a haircut" applies to these lettered merchants of hope.

The problem is easily seen in a typical equity fund that replicates a major stock market index. If the index, say the Dow Jones Industrial Average, has an average 2.6 percent dividend yield and the advisor's fees are 2.5 percent, what's left is erosion of 0.1 percent of the annual dividend. If the fund thrives and its units rise a few dollars a year, the investor may be pleased. But without the dividend, he or she has been engaged in pure price speculation. Stocks wobble, but large company dividends tend to be dependable and, often, rise at a pleasant pace. The same index packed in an exchange traded fund with a 0.20 percent annual management fee would leave a 2.4 percent annual dividend for growth. That's valuable protection in the chaos of the market.

The effect of fees is even more drastic in the bond market, where yields have recently been in low single digits with little prospect of rising and much likelihood of falling. One needs bonds in a balanced portfolio, but in a market in which the odds are stacked against the investor, low fees and a very discriminating guide are essential. The investor, even a neophyte properly worried about loss, must ask what the advisor hopes to deliver for the money.

WHO WINS AND WHO DIES — IT'S A QUESTION OF TIMING

The easiest demonstration of the ways of the financial world is a look at the back of performance. A particular fund or portfolio will have gained some amount over various periods. No doubt, but the wider question is what all the portfolios of a manager or management company have done over many periods when markets have been up, down, and gone sideways. Large fund companies will have scores, perhaps hundreds, of individually named portfolios, and it is inevitable that a few will thrive no matter what. If you see the advertisements for fund manager X saying that its global bond fund or North American stock fund has beaten rivals and the index for one, two, three, and five years, ask about other periods. Ask about other funds they manage. The rule in investments is that the goal posts, where one starts and stops, establish performance. With that in mind, even the worst fund can be made to look good and the best of funds look bad for selective periods. Worse, there is the problem of managed death of unsuccessful funds that are merged into more popular or better performing funds. This is called "survivor bias," and it is the unknown and seldom mentioned problem that the worst of the worst, the truly hopeless that no one but a financial masochist would buy, are put to death.[6] Thus, lists of funds for sale are lists of those that have done well enough to be kept in business. The wretched funds, the hopeless portfolio of bad picks and perhaps bad management, have been made to disappear.

The survivor bias problem is pervasive in life, for what we see and read and feel is the world of the living.[7] For example, if you take the characteristics of the founders of Apple Inc. and Microsoft Corp., you find that both were college dropouts whose businesses changed the world. Does that mean dropping out of college is a path to riches? Hardly. But we do not have comprehensive numbers for dropouts who failed. This is a critical omission. As an investment process, the criteria for successful companies described in Tom Peters and Robert H. Waterman Jr.'s 1982 global bestseller *In Search of Excellence*, of thirty-five companies that were described as global leaders and that had easily trackable publicly traded stocks, need to be studied with a magnifying glass. It is worth noting that twenty have underperformed the market average since the book's publication. Among the early 1980s outperformers are NCR Corp., Wang Labs, and Xerox. NCR did very well up to 2007, then subsided to good but not exciting performance. Xerox thrived in the dot-com period, hit US$63 in 1999, then subsided to about US$27, give or take. Wang filed for bankruptcy in 1992.

What is wrong with hot market theories is that you, the investor, are not there. Peters and Waterman were accused of fiddling with their data by critics. We'll give full credit to the authors for excellent scholarship and flawless honesty (why not?), but — this is the point — they did not test the traits of successful companies against others with the same traits such as "decide fast" (that is, don't research and conference a thing to death) and "be close to the customer" (that is, don't treat clients as numbers and fail to return calls). Statistically, they omitted testing residual variables, which may have been as important as the ones they found to be valid. The authors did not search for companies with the same set of qualities that failed. By analogy, we could say that successful businesses use arithmetic or have elevators. The response, of course, is "So what?" In the end, in our view, admiring success at a distance is less valuable than being there.

Survivorship can be seen in a pyramid of coins that are successively flipped. Start with 64 perfect dimes and flip them. Half, or 32, should come up heads. Flip again, and 16 of the original batch will still be heads. Then 8 come up heads, et cetera. The last dime to have come up heads in every flip is the winner, a great coin destined for great things. Of course, barring the possibility — which we excluded by assuming that all the coins are perfect — that the survivor was weighted on the tails side so that the head would be more likely to be facing up, the outcome was merely inevitable. It would have been stupid to bet on any dime in the process. The opening odds of any dime going through seven flips and staying heads every time were 64 to 1, but in life, the cost of play would have made a fair bet impossible. Betting on every dime would have left you poorer than when you started, for every game of chance has some explicit or implicit cost of play.

The survivor bias problem is clear in this bit of math but unquantifiable in capital markets. One can always see companies that thrive. Taking their characteristics as essentials for business or profit is only half the analysis. What is just as important is finding out what the flops did not have that the winners did.

Companies with the same characteristics that did not make it are not visible without much research. Thus, knowing the losers and what made them fail is vital if you give your money to the companies whose stock you buy. Theory alone is not the answer. Knowing what is in your portfolio can be the difference between success and getting wiped out.

> One can always see companies that thrive, but what is just as important is finding out what the flops did not have that the winners did.

Paradoxically, survivor bias is rife among financial advisors. They seldom want to reveal that their collective performance is whatever the gods of finance and the brains of managers can make happen. Some are hot dimes, for that is inevitable. But of the coins, or advisors, in any of the reduction sequences, none has any real edge on the next iteration of flips. Fees, which eat up performance, are constant. The manager with a conscience has to beat the market. But the odds are with low fees and no selection at all in broad index funds. This truth is known in the financial community but seldom told to neophyte investors. On the other hand, the investor with time and a taste for learning, starting with what is known and moving to unfamiliar fields over time, has an edge they can exploit.

Intervening in one's own affairs could seem odd. We trust our physicians to produce good diagnoses without asking how this or that lab test works or what qualifications a specialist has to poke at us. But financial planning is different. Credentials are easy to get, there is a compromise between aiding the client and fattening the advisor's wallet or the employer's, and if the outcomes are bad, the advisor can blame the client for being hasty to sell or impatient not to wait out the market. Bottom line: Do what you know, not what somebody else with a spiel or some fancy numbers says will work. And always ask why any tale should come out with a gain for you. You can use your own good sense to question claims that stocks are headed for new highs or will recover from dreadful lows.

The basic question is why anyone would buy a product. At the level of companies that sell groceries, a trip to the store to chat with a manager is a good beginning. If you are considering buying an automobile maker, visit showrooms, look at the models, read the car press, and then read analysts' reports. Want to buy a baby carriage maker or a bicycle company? Start with the people who sell the things. Ask about quality, competition, pricing, and performance. When you get to the analysts' reports, your shoe leather research will be all the more relevant and meaningful.

This approach is old-fashioned, but it works as the foundation of choice. It is true that many analysts who do quantitative analysis and shop only by numbers skip this basic form of research. But the quants, as they are called, take refuge in numbers. They may have scores or hundreds of stocks in their portfolios. Shoe leather research is impossible. But for the beginner eager to avoid losses, it is vital. The goal is to build lasting wealth. If you think of your portfolio as a corner store and ask what products are selling, which are not, why each is true, and where the profits are made, you will be on your way to building a successful portfolio.

CHAPTER 1

Crowds: There Is Wisdom in Collective Judgment, but Tragedy Lurks

In some arcane fields of economics and political science, in the concept of having a jury decide the fate of an accused, and in statistical sampling of opinions, the idea that many players can reach the right decision by consensus gets a lot of respect. It is quite different in the relatively mundane arena of trading assets for profit. Often, where crowds go, the individual should not.

To be on the ground floor of a stock before it soars is good. And to be first to sell before it plummets is terrific, for selling is usually harder than buying. The problem for almost every investor is that what the crowd does influences your buy or sell decision. If the stock is going up, that is a buy signal for those who see hope. When the stock price is falling, some will figure that the asset is on sale — a time to buy. The impetus to sell on price movements is the opposite of buying fruit at the supermarket. When the price of apples falls, you may want to buy more; when the price rises, you may buy less. But here the connection to stocks and other assets breaks. After all — and this is the crucial point — you are unlikely to try to resell your apples. Fruit is a one-way decision, unlike stocks, which have an implicit sell concept every time you buy and even a repurchase notion when you sell.

We don't make investment buy or sell decisions independently of the market. Even so-called quants, the managers and investors who juggle numerous variables on their computers to make trading decisions, have to take notice of what others are doing. When the others are part of a stock heading from nothing to the heavens, many observe, want to join the party for fear of being left out, and become part of the problem that, good or bad, assets can become bubbles. And when bubbles are pricked, the path to safety can lead to the abyss of loss.

The problem for almost every investor is that what the crowd does influences your buy or sell decision.

The irrationality of chasing bubbles is clear in the mirror of a small store owner's inventory management. If an owner of a dress shop sees a competitor down the block selling out of a certain kind of garment, would it be wise to order as many as possible of it so that they could flood the street with more of the same? Doubtful. Dresses have styles and styles have their day, and one competitor's stock of frocks isn't tradeable information. Basing your own buy or sell decisions on the trend rather than the substance is the foundation of bubble madness.

BUBBLES AND CROWDS

The difference between a singularly individual decision and a rush to trade because others are doing it is the problem of crowdthink. In investment markets — the crowd, that is, the mass of investors — by definition stays with the trend. The crowd embraces the wisdom of the moment or, if you like, the convictions of the moment. But trading with the crowd really requires timing. It amounts to trying to time a popularity contest. Errors in underpricing a stock or bond, real estate parcel, or other asset can persist as long as those errors overpricing the same asset. In short, you can observe a bubble or even a trend you think is wrong. The right thing to do is to either trade the other way or ignore what you think is foolishness. Chasing the rainbow is not a good option. Understanding it is quite another matter.

If you dismiss the stock market as collective paranoia, you miss its greatest virtue — over time, with diversified investments, it pays a very nice return. For the very long period from 1802 to 2002, U.S. stocks produced an average annual return of 6.6 percent, almost twice the 3.6 percent average annual return of bonds in the same period. Gold had an average annual return of 0.7 percent over those two centuries. Cash suffered a 1.4 percent average annual inflation-driven loss of buying power in the period.[1] The market cannot exist without a range of estimates of value from dour to wildly enthusiastic, but the investor has to find a path through the emotional chaff to get to the wheat. Clearly, holding for the long run is worth it.

> If you dismiss the stock market as collective paranoia, you miss its greatest virtue — over time, with diversified investments, it pays a very nice return.

Crowds drive stocks. Every major company on an exchange has thousands of holders, and very big stocks have tens of thousands. Emotion drives much stock trading activity whether the assets are dullards or demons. The investor can use tools to judge the level of enthusiasm — trading volume, for example — but it is essential to trade against the crowd, not with it. That is the simple wisdom of buying low when others don't covet a stock, and selling high when they do. Put another way, the market lives on liquidity, and crowds provide that liquidity. For the investor, who is part of liquidity, survival requires reason, as well as enthusiasm, to get into a stock and a strong sense of when the crowd has gone too far in its enthusiasm or despair. The moral: Watch the crowd, but don't be part of it. In stock investing, independence not only pays, but is also a safety switch.

Herd instinct or groupthink identifies the tendency of people to follow trends. It is a wish to belong, to be part of the movement that is being either smart to get in or smart to get out. It is the pressure to conform or to belong or to be part of what is happening. When these pressures supplant the investor's own thinking or what should be his or her analysis of a potential investment or sale, then the imbalance grows, with emotion replacing reason. It sounds very theoretical, but it has happened in the past — the dot-coms of the late 1990s, for example — and it is happening as this chapter is being written. The price-to-earnings ratios of such digital darlings as Netflix Inc., which is at 234, and Amazon.com Inc., at 254, are measures of frenzy, not foundations for stable growth. Each stock may reward its holders handsomely if its profits rise to the occasion. It can happen and perhaps will, but for Netflix, for example, to fall to a p/e of, say, twenty would require that earnings rise by 1,000 percent while the share price does not budge. Neither process is likely. Investors in Netflix or Amazon may be handsomely rewarded for their patience or bravery, but the odds are that each company's exceptional growth will subside and that late entrants will suffer losses. That is the price of late arrival to a fad.

The mechanism of crowd enthusiasm has been called the bandwagon effect. As the stock's price rises, the shares go from being classed as value investments with p/e ratios of six or so to perhaps twenty, to growth investments with p/e ratios up to forty, and then momentum shares with p/e valuations up to the hundreds. Investors dream of getting in when p/e's are low and getting out when they are high. The problem, of course, is finding where the party starts and knowing when it is prudent to leave.

It isn't easy to quit the game when the talk around the water cooler or in the coffee shop is about how, this time, it will be different. It isn't different, though. Small upstream oil drillers with stocks that seem to rocket off single-digit price bases just as readily fall. Example: Global upstream oil and gas companies slashed expenditures by 40 percent between 2014 and 2016 and laid off 400,000 workers.[2]

These survival moves may have protected future profitability, but the layoffs made the companies smaller and many of their stocks worth less. Investors abandoned shares of such firms as Baytex Energy Corp., which traded at almost $50 in mid-2014 and subsequently fell to $4.29 in June 2018. The company's earnings have shriveled, and the stock at today's price is a bargain if oil prices rise substantially. So far, investors are not taking the bet. Contrarian sentiment is absent.

It works both ways. There is a fundamental social urge to want to join a party, to be part of a movement, or to get in on something others have. The more a stock's price rises, the greater the pressure to join. If the stock's price rises high enough, as shown by Amazon.com Inc.'s trailing p/e of 270, the pressure to get into the miracle can be irresistible. No matter that Amazon has no dividends; it was a mere US$400 at the start of 2015. As this chapter is being written, Amazon's price is US$1,681. It could go higher, of course, and Amazon appears to be eating the retail world. However, with this p/e, if earnings — just US$4 per share — were to drop by one dollar, the effect would be to drive the price of the stock down by US$270. The risk of going in at this valu-ation is apparent. Yet daily volume in Amazon is 1.3 million shares. Some hold-ers are selling, of course, but for every share sold, there is a buyer. For now, there seems no limit to how high Amazon shares can rise.

> The divide between good investments and disasters waiting to happen is the quality of decision making.

One day, it will change. Amazon is, after all, just a phase of retailing. There were bricks and mortar depart-ment stores before Amazon, and then combo stores called "clicks and mortar," which covered traditional retailers that also sell online. For non-physical services, the web is the ideal platform. The limits on sales are conceptual, not physical, but even concepts have their day. It is perhaps too soon to know how far virtual stores can go selling virtual products. It is good to have a foot in the door, for there is no doubt share prices will rise even though the metrics of the industry are not yet mature. In other words, we do not know what analysts and other investors will think important in a decade or two. But new businesses create their own measures. When the dot-coms were new and anything with a dot or a com in the name was hot, the metrics of value included how fast the companies burned up their capital. This was seen as a good thing, even though for most firms the idea and goal is to build up capital, not to destroy it. Fashions come and go. Capital burn was a bad idea then and, in retrospect, ridiculous.

The issue and the divide between good investments and disasters waiting to happen is the quality of decision making. Here we can refer to studies on peer pressure. Seminal studies of group versus individual thinking show that people in groups focused on a problem are more productive when they ponder on their own than when they cerebrate together.[3] An experiment proves the point. Between 1951 and 1956, a psychologist named Solomon Asch conducted experiments on the dangers of group influence. He gathered student volunteers into groups and asked them to take a vision test. He showed them a picture of three lines of varying lengths and asked how the lines compared to each other. The question was simple, and 95 percent of students were able to rank lines from shortest to longest and determine which matched others. But when Asch planted actors in the groups who confidently gave incorrect answers, as he had instructed them to do, only 25 percent of the volunteers gave correct answers. The other 75 percent went along with the misguiding volunteers.[4]

CROWD MENTALITY

The urge to get into a hot stock is a form of groupthink. That urge not to be left behind can be stimulated by stories in the press, by good news planted by corporate public relations departments, and by confected stories that a fund or famous investor can't take on any new clients. That was the modus operandi of Bernard Madoff, who, with a reported US$52 billion overstatement of assets, is the biggest crook of all time.

Madoff's technique was not to beat the drum for his funds; rather, he told prospective investors that he could not possibly take their money. It became a contest among the wealthy to get in. He identified the bandwagon effect and raised the gate for entry. Refusal of fresh money was only a gambit, for he took as much as he could. As with a restaurant in Manhattan known for exotic prices and snotty waiters, reservations a month in advance backed by a credit card, and the threat of charge for not showing up, the barriers to entry were the enticement. This was reverse psychology applied as a sales technique. And it worked.

What Madoff did was to add roadblocks, and that made his game all the more prestigious. Results were unusual in that he claimed to have steady returns of 8 percent a year in and out of good and bad times. Such returns with almost no variation can be achieved with perfect options tactics, but that is very difficult to do and highly improbable. Corporate finance experts doubted his record was real and communicated their concerns to the U.S. Securities and Exchange Commission, and the SEC ignored the warnings.

The great bubbles in history include the Dutch tulip mania of 1634 to 1637, the British South Sea Company of 1720, the French confection called the Mississippi Company of the same year, the global stock inflation of the 1920s, the Japanese property bubble of the 1980s, the dot-com bubble of 1998 to 2000, and of course the great mortgage flop that ended in 2008 with the evaporation of trillions of dollars of debt wealth that had been built on mortgages that should never have been issued and that wound up in default.

> Bubbles are diverse in place, time, and substance, but all have the same element — the desire among outsiders to get in.

The biggest Canadian flop was Nortel Networks, shares of which were, at the beginning of the millennium, a third of the total value of all stocks listed on the Toronto Stock Exchange. Shares peaked on July 26, 2000, at $124.50, which would be the equivalent of about $210 in today's terms after inflation. Shares were worth just 39 cents before bankruptcy filing on January 14, 2009. What had propelled Nortel to the position of the biggest stock in Canada was not only the rush of investors to get in, but also the reluctance of fund managers to miss out. After all, press reports called Nortel "the centre of the universe," and sheer momentum investing was evidence of people piling into the hottest stock in the land. It was a large cap behaving like a small cap gold mine that had just hit a vein of ore that, no matter how improbable it seemed, would not even need refining. On October 24, 2000, Nortel shares had the first of what would become many major tumbles, plummeting after revenue growth missed the company target. In 2009, Nortel filed for bankruptcy and its shares were delisted by the Toronto Stock Exchange.

These bubbles are diverse in place, time, and substance. But all have the same consistent element — the desire among outsiders to get in. Early participants see their stakes soar, the process is glamourized in the press, outsiders figure that they must not miss the boat to financial paradise, and then it all ends with massive losses.

Crowdthink is not limited to suckers throwing their life savings into improbable small caps. The rich do it, too. The Madoff scandal was unusual in that it spared almost no one who gave Madoff money, but it, of course, was an engineered flop peddled to the affluent who wanted nothing more than stable returns.

Madoff's victims included Elie Wiesel, winner of the Nobel Peace Prize in 1986, and many charities. All believed in the Madoff gimmick of steady though unspectacular returns. The investors were risk averters yet unwittingly took on the huge risk of fraud. Madoff's financial statements were superficially proper, but in the details there were clues. The Madoff funds were audited by a man deep into his Social Security years in a tiny office in a suburban strip mall. Ironically, when critics of the business asked regulators to look in, nothing was done. So the con went on until the contradictions were too large to be ignored. Madoff ran out of money to give to clients who wanted to cash out. Then the walls came tumbling down. It was a bubble that, in the end, few had dared to deflate.

THE ODD ECONOMICS OF CROWDS

The bandwagon effect has companion irrational pricing behaviours, each of which an investor should sense and then avoid.

The snob effect. People buy into an idea, a product, or an investment because it is rare or not widely owned. A price tag of seven figures for Andy Warhol's soap boxes or soup cans is not based on the intrinsic value of a copy of a box or can; it is an entry into a community sharing an idea. Buyers are to be seen as clever for having gotten the irony. And rich enough to buy into the concept.

Prestige pricing. In February 2015, a painting of two Tahitian girls by Paul Gaugin was sold, reportedly to a museum in Qatar, for US$300 million. That price was surpassed by the sale of a picture called *Salvator Mundi* thought to have been painted by Leonardo da Vinci. The price as reported was US$450 million. Doubts were expressed as to its authenticity as a da Vinci, but we'll accept that it is the real thing.[5] However, price and even rarity do not make it more valuable than

Rembrandts hanging on museum walls, destined never to be sold and, therefore, technically priceless. With no active market in the greatest works of art, prestige rather than sale sets price. People admire the da Vinci in part because it is expensive. Were it priced at, say, $1 million, it would be just another fine picture — very nice, but not quite breathtaking. And at $30, if you can imagine that, it would be motel art. What people admire is not only the image and the remarkable virtuosity of the artist, but the price as well.

Inverse pricing. Fancy Swiss watches are sold as "aspirational"; that is, if you have one, you can say you have arrived. Thus, a real Rolex or Patek Philippe with a five-figure price is a symbol of prosperity. It shows that you have a fat wallet. Or it may show that you are foolish with your money. If the fancy watch did not have a high price, it would not be so desirable. In theory, we admire those who strap lovely timepieces to their wrists, but that admiration is for the name and perhaps the gold, for a $100 digital watch keeps better time than the $100,000-or-more Swiss job with "complications" that can show moonrise on the other side of the planet. In theory, everybody would like one of these, never mind the insurance cost — often 1 percent to 3 percent per year of appraised value — just to walk around with the thing. If you paid $40,000 for the nice gold Rolex, the annual insurance tab could be as much as $1,200. In functional terms, buying one of these puppies is irrational. The point is, the watch with a six- or even seven-figure price tag is not just a time piece. It is a badge of belonging. It is the corollary of the theory of Thorstein Veblen, a Swedish American economist and author of *The Theory of the Leisure Class* (1899), an academic bestseller that served to limit the idea that falling prices boost quantity demanded of any good or service. Rising prices attract sales in the Parisian famousname designer business where the name of the house establishes the price range. High price indicates desirability in this part of the demand curve. Usually, declining price makes things more desirable. But fancy frocks are not conventional goods. They are more like the hottest fad stocks. Curiously, neither are permanent. The $30,000 dress custom beaded by a flock of grannies will be last season's fashion in months. A glamour stock, as Facebook or Amazon is today, could hold its value, but history shows either stocks work up earnings to justify their three-digit p/e ratios, which seldom happens, or their prices fall, which is usually what happens. Nothing goes up forever.

Getting in on a hot stock or perhaps piece of real estate is the crux of the matter. It explains why people toss money at high-priced stocks. Note that the trading price is not an expression of value. Were there a split, there would be twice as many shares at half the price.

Recently high-priced stocks include Berkshire Hathaway Inc. (share price: US$302,000, give or take), Seaboard Corp. (share price: US$3,638), and Priceline Group Inc. (share price: US$1,905). There are many more, but each is a showpiece for a founder and a sneer at the yokels who did not buy early. The share price creates lack of liquidity. On that basis, it is a bad thing, yet the high price is also a marquee for management. After all, if Warren Buffett's Berkshire Hathaway were a $10 stock, where would the glamour be? It would be just another holding company, and a cheap one at that. A form of bandwagon effect has propelled Berkshire Hathaway into the stratosphere of stock prices. There is no more expensive American share, and no investor more esteemed than Warren Buffett. His stock price attests to his acumen. The fact that a single share of Berkshire Hathaway trades at about US$290,000 at time of writing makes it a kind of destination investment for everybody. The fact that Mr. Buffett is the biggest owner of Berkshire Hathaway, along with his partner, Los Angeles lawyer Charlie Munger, adds to the glamour. The fact that the stock pays no dividend is, well, just something to live with. You can get a better return on equity — for Berkshire's is just 5 percent or so — from hundreds of other stocks. Trading is only a couple of hundred shares a day. This is not only deliberately priced for glamour, even though one can buy Berkshire baby shares at about US$190 as this chapter is being written, but the biggest cachet, given that Mr. Buffett is an octogenarian, is that the owner can say that he or she was there with the great man. This may be bandwagon investing, but it's a bandwagon with solid support.

> History shows either stocks work up earnings to justify their three-digit p/e ratios, which seldom happens, or their prices fall, which is usually what happens.

The Berkshire Hathaway phenomenon underlies the paradox of all investments in shares and, for that matter, most real estate, bonds, gems, paintings, and even antique farm machinery. Where value is either something embedded in a stock for accountants to work out or, in functional terms, very low for a functioning but rusty ancient tractor, the intrinsic price is different from the market price. The latter is always some expression of cost of production. The cost of production of Andy Warhol's commercial product imitations was surely less than a hundred bucks each. That they are esteemed by collectors says a lot about the collectors and nothing about the soap boxes. Likewise, holding a stock that pays no dividend that would give it some intrinsic value as a fixed income asset is a bet on the future and what others will pay for it. Crowdthink is with us and irreplaceable. The problem for the investor is to judge when the crowd is right, too timid, or too enthusiastic.

CROWD JUDGMENT ANALYZED

John Maynard Keynes likened the process of investing to picking the prettiest girl in a beauty contest. "It is not to pick the prettiest girl, but to pick the girl the majority of other judges will think prettiest," he said. And so we come to the problem of separating fundamental price from the groupthink premium or deduction. This is the foundation of making sound investment decisions and knowing both when to buy and when to sell.

Let's admit that there are no fixed rules. A stock priced at fifty times earnings expected next year could be a reasonable buy or a fool's rush to loss. Selling when a stock has fallen to six times earnings or even less, or a no-p/e situation where there are no earnings, may be a wise bet on recovery or utter idiocy. A low p/e may indicate a bargain or a truly hopeless stock nobody wants. But a p/e in the hundreds indicates herd instinct. Enthusiasm tends to get ahead of earnings growth. You have to investigate.

In engineering terms, stock booms are often examples of feedback loops, with one movement echoed by others, each move up supported by recent moves. It works the opposite on the way down, of course. In the feedback process, analysts and investors progressively ignore fundamentals in favour of the popularity or unpopularity trend — more people are buying in or leaving. Literally, crowd behaviour induces people to take leave of their senses.

It's possible to analyze stock or other asset price moves statistically. If prices rise in the fashion of a parabola with a positive rate of increase, then peak as the rate of increase declines, the effect of mob investment may be at the top. Similarly, if price on the way down resembles an upside-down parabola, when the decline levels off it may be time to get in if the stock on its merits is attractive. All this assumes that stock prices will trace smooth curves. Seldom is that the case. However, it is true that no stock can have a dramatic rise forever. If it did, it would be worth more than all the other stocks in the world combined. Nor can it have an endless drive downward. Once it hits zero, it can lose no more. Pure numerical analysis tells nothing about the peak and trough, but good sense should suggest to the investor that the influence of groupthink has to weaken as either top or bottom approaches. Were it not so, the trend would continue forever. And that has never happened.

> Stock booms are often examples of feedback loops, with one movement echoed by others, each move up supported by recent moves.

Finding tops and bottoms can be aided by the rules of so-called technical analysis. Plot the price, look at the trendlines and the various 90-, 180-, and 270-day moving averages, and if the stock is far below the averages, consider a buy. If far above, consider a sell. This is a form of simple price arbitrage — you sell the winners and you buy the losers. In a graphical sense, all technical analysis is backward looking, and all of it presumes that what is known is summed up in price lines. All of that is true, but none of it can account for new information such as higher earnings or a downer like the company president's indictment for corporate crime. Moreover, technical analysis tries to map share prices and trading volume and other variables into visual representations. If the period expands from a day to a yearly average, lots of volatility disappears. Move to a ten-year moving weekly average, which is the sum of 520 weeks divided by 520, and there is not much wobble. With twenty-year moving weekly averages, with the sum of prices for 1,040 weeks divided by 1,040, only the trend is visible. What is wrong with such long averages is that they challenge our wish to live in the present. And if you invest on margin with money borrowed from your investment dealer or perhaps on a personal loan from your bank secured against your house, a home equity line of credit, interest can eat you up before you see a profit.

MICRO KNOWLEDGE
VERSUS MACRO UNDERSTANDING

The stock market and indeed many other asset markets are said to be paranoid, jumping up on good news and plummeting on bad news. In periods of minutes or hours, perhaps days and even a week or two after good or bad news, asset prices tend to show large, sympathetic movements. But over longer periods, the prices of individual stocks move in a similar proportion to each other. Over periods of years, stock prices move in proper relation to input costs, foreign competition, and taxation. Investors tend to move in blocks as well, buying the perceived winners and dumping the losers. For example, shares of the Finnish phone maker Nokia Corp., traded on the New York Stock Exchange, were at US$50 in 2000 when Nokia dominated the cellular handset market. Today, with the smart phone revolution having largely passed Nokia by, its shares are trading at about US$5.80. In the same period, shares of Apple Inc. have moved up from US$4 to US$185. Apple shares, which sold at US$28.45 at the beginning of 2008, lost about half their value in the great meltdown in 2008, falling to $13.25 in 2009, but have recovered and gained price to many times the value of the previous peak. Simply buying low and selling high would have made the investor a tidy fortune. But going with the crowd and selling on momentum when the stock was falling and buying on sympathetic enthusiasm when it was rising was the wrong strategy. The right move was to trade against the crowd. The point is that an investor doing Apple trades his or her own way could have beaten the enthusiasm of momentum traders who were part of the crowd. The prize went to trading against the mob.

OF LONGS AND SHORTS

Good stocks can be overbought and bad ones oversold. For the overbought good stock, perhaps a market darling, as mines and oil wells are from time to time, cyclical enthusiasm has its own cure in the inevitable correction. Short sellers try to get ahead of declines by selling shares they think ripe for a fall. They work opposite to those who prefer to buy low and sell high. The shorts, as they are called in market lingo, just do it backwards.

> That one can make a lot of money on a crummy stock should make one realize there is money in being a contrarian.

The stock to be sold is borrowed from those who have it, usually insurance companies. When the tumble has happened or even if the stock has risen, the shorts buy the stock and return the borrowed shares to the insurance companies or other investors. But it does not always work, and the shorts, who may find that they have to pay more for stock than the price at which they sold it, can be cleaned out as surely as if they bought for too much and wound up seeing their shares plummet.

However, there is a mechanism for short covering, and it can make tidy profits for those who hold shares they are holding for sale. To save their skins, the shorts have to buy. The short-covering rally will force the price of the stock upward. It is momentum that makes these plays work. Moreover, that one can make a lot of money on a crummy stock, either as a short hoping for a drop or from a long position if the stock improves with debt reduction or rising earnings, should make one realize that there is money in being a contrarian.

In 2008, as overvalued credit pyramids, particularly those made up of credit obligations based on other credit obligations, fell apart, a few speculators cashed in and made billions even though big banks, notably Deutsche Bank, had viewed the credit pyramids as absolutely solid. DB had created securities to enable the shorts to trade, then found itself on the wrong side of the deals. DB's loss was estimated at US$3.1 billion. To pay it, DB had to sell its New York office tower.[6] There were predictions that the crisis would take down UBS, Merrill

Lynch, Deutsche Bank, Bank of America, and HSBC. None did fail, but all suffered huge drops in their stock prices. Royal Bank of Scotland lost a reported US$15.2 billion, and its chief deal maker, Sir Fred Goodwin, lost his title for his role in the mess.[7] In September 1992, the financier George Soros bet that the Bank of England could not support the pound, which he regarded as overvalued against other currencies in the European Exchange Rate Mechanism — a process designed to hold currencies in certain bands relative to others. The ERM failed, the Bank of England caved and took a £3.4 billion loss, and Soros walked away with what was reported as a US$1 billion profit. Playing with the crowd may work for a time, but playing against it can make for even larger gains.

ANALYSTS IN THE HYPE

Stock analysts make handsome livings examining company operations in fine detail. Each industry has its own metrics. What works for insurance does not necessarily apply to airlines. But every analyst observes the consensus, remembers that his or her employer may be doing investment banking for the company under review, and acts accordingly. Analysts tend to a consensus and even may refuse to admit major revisions. Gold mining analysts continued to believe that the purported results of Bre-X Minerals Ltd., which had been hyped as the biggest gold find in the world, were valid even after it became clear that much of the operation was a fraud,. The core of Bre-X cheerleaders could not accept that the biggest gold mine in the world, and perhaps the biggest ever, was a total fake. The fraud hit big pension funds, sector funds that had to have a piece of Bre-X, mutual fund managers whose unitholders insisted they get into Bre-X, countless small investors, and the idea that democracy can assess asset values.

What happened, of course, is that the careful cynicism of early investors in Bre-X had given way to the feeling among investors that they had to buy in lest they miss the boat. Analysts cheered each other on with increasing estimates of gold in the ground going from thirty million metric ounces in 1995 to seventy million ounces in 1997. Equity funds with

Canadian gold companies in their mandates had to buy. Bre-X was institutionalized in gold indexes. That expanded the market. The company's endless announcements that ever more gold was being found turned careful investors into cheerleaders.

The Bre-X shares soared to C$296.50 adjusted for splits by May 1996, with a total capitalization of C$6 billion. The company collapsed the next year when it was found that samples given to analysts were a fraud. They were salted with alluvial gold from river beds that could not have been in core samples. Yet before it unravelled, major engineering consultants had verified the lode. Analysts who were supposed to be skeptics gave up, though some admitted that no one had seen actual core samples of the rocks alleged to contain gold. An American mining giant, Freeport-McMoRan, in the process of evaluating Bre-X for a buyout, reported that there was no gold. The roof fell in.

Emotion had surpassed reason when looking at the fundamentals and the idea that if you want to rig up a gold fraud, there is no better place to do it than in a forbidding jungle in Indonesia. The descent from grace was blamed on an obscure geologist from the Philippines, Mike de Guzman, who reportedly fell or jumped out of a helicopter over the jungle. What was supposedly his body was found a few days later severely decomposed and partially eaten by wild boars. It was swiftly cremated, and no dental impressions were taken to verify that the corpse was de Guzman. The purported remains were just a quarter mile from a logging road and confirmed by another geologist who said he knew de Guzman. The principals at Bre-X retired, and investors were the poorer for their understandable sin of accepting that the mob of investors just could not be wrong. But they were. In the end, major pension funds and small investors were victims of believing that the masses throwing money into Bre-X could not be mistaken.

Bre-X declared bankruptcy in November 1997. The Ontario Securities Commission charged John Felderhof, a senior officer of the company, with some technical offences, including insider trading. After years of litigation, Felderhof was found not guilty. The whole affair had been pulled off, it was said, by the now dead geologist from the Philippines. Incredibly, this is not where it ends. One obscure geologist who had, it was reported, numerous wives to support was given the credit — really the blame — for conning the world's gold mining analysts, investors, securities regulators, much of the salivating press, and the officers of Bre-X. It was groupthink validating the biggest gold bubble in history. A few years later it was reported that one of the geologist's wives had received a hefty cheque from her supposedly dead husband.[8] In retrospect, that was one of the less amazing facts in this episode of mass intoxication with greed.

To have been a skeptic of Bre-X early in the stock's ascent was unwise. Brokers wanted to sell shares. Existing shareholders wanted more shares. Outsiders had to get in. That the mine was on the other side of the world, in a remote jungle with snakes and not very friendly natives, inaccessible to all but the most intrepid, and that the company did not provide the customary core samples — all that was ignored. It was a pot of gold that allowed enthusiasm to overcome reason. Unbelievers and holdouts were not welcome at the party. For the professional investors and analysts who took part, the money from in-and-out trading that begat big commissions and short-term profits, as well as the lavish press stories, was too good to ignore.

> Given the tendency of analysts to be bullish, an investor is wise to seek opinions from disinterested sources.

WHO CAN YOU TRUST?

Given the tendency of analysts to be bullish, lest they offend the investment bankers in their firm, an investor is wise to seek opinions from disinterested sources. Outside analysts — data services such as Reuters, bond rating services such as Standard & Poor's and the Canadian DBRS (formerly Dominion Bond Rating Service), press reports, and analysts reports, tainted though they may be — can provide a sense of the possible and perhaps a warning of the impossible. Consensus is no guarantee, nor is deviance from the consensus. Remember that most analysts thought the American energy fraud Enron was a legitimate operation long after its off-balance-sheet trickery was exposed. In sensing what is right and wrong, you don't need to be accurate. If you sense a rat even though the majority of analysts and bullish investors like the stock or asset, just move on. For most people, the psychic cost of not being in a hot stock is less than the remorse from jumping in and losing. The reason is not just hurt feelings. After all, a loss of any amount is a greater fraction of the wealth diminished by the loss than of the wealth one had before the loss occurred.

> For most people, the psychic cost of not being in a hot stock is less than the remorse from jumping in and losing.

Trading volume should be an indicator of activity; unfortunately, it is not. When volume on a small cap picks up, it is a significant indicator. On a mid- to large-cap stock, it may mean more pair trades, in which an institutional trader buys some of one thing — say, a steel company — and then shorts shares of another steel company. The volume of trades is doubled, but it is only because an investor or fund manager has decided to be on both sides of a trend. If news helps steels, he can close out the short. If it hurts steels, he'll close the long position and ride the short.

There are no hard and fast rules on comparison of market price to asset price. Investors used to regard the price movements of a day or a month or even a quarter as mere noise. Today, with holding periods for shares averaging just a few days, courtesy of the dominance of actively traded investment funds in the market, there are, in a sense, two worlds: fast swaps on wisps of information or rumours in one world, and in the other world, long-term value.

The fashion for trading on instant information has been exacerbated by the internet, to which information is swiftly sent and often swiftly forgotten. Social media, chat rooms, and the incessant drone of financial TV provide information and kindle enthusiasm. Fear and greed, variously the mourners and cheerleaders of investment analysis, have turned the process of buying a stock or bond or chunk of real estate into a mob game. The trick for the individual investor is to see the fundamentals. Above all, invest for your needs and expectations — the simplest concept of what you may get, not what others, some seeking commissions, may puff up from notion to almost tangible reality. In law, there is a saying: He who acts through another acts himself. It is the starting point of the law of agency, but — this is the point — you are always the person whose wallet is on the line. What the crowd does is noise. Your own wisdom and pencil work are what count.

We have to make a distinction between enthusiasm, what Keynes called "animal spirits" in his *General Theory of Employment, Interest and Money*, published in 1936, and the euphoria that goes with the irresistible urge to get in on a trend or a hot stock. In the process, investment on rational lines based on expected profits and dividends turns to faith in rising price, and that faith spreads and is self-reinforcing. When a price peaks, perhaps because the mob of investors has run out of money or because some spark of reality enters the equation, the mob tries to flee.

Walter Bagehot, founder of *The Economist* and a great theorist of nineteenth-century central banking, described the process when writing of the crisis of 1814: "The frenzy, I can call it nothing less ... descended to persons in the humblest circumstances ... not only clerks and labourers, but menial servants, engaged the little sums which they had been laying up for a provision against old age and sickness ... [then] the poor dupes of the delusion has lost their little hoards and went on the parish [relief]."[9] Worse, some who lost may have been sent to Victorian workhouses; that is, pay-to-stay jails for the poor.

FRESH FUEL FOR BUBBLES

The antidote for the lure of the mob is reasoned valuation. Looking at trading in a small stock with relatively few shares trading, there is not much opportunity for mass trading. Daily volume of shares excludes institutions and high-velocity traders. The stock may have good dividends and good prospects, but there is too little of it to sustain any mob trading. At the other extreme, a major stock like IBM or Apple has all the float any high-velocity trader may want. The restraint to runaway buying or selling is the vast amount held by investment funds, pension funds, and exchange traded funds.

Much groupthink can be seen driving penny stocks. The reasons are cheap entry, traders' ability to buy a lot of it for little, and the potential for huge gains on small bases. The most fertile area for group pressure is the category of microcaps, defined as stocks with perhaps no more than $250 million total value being traded on the stock market. They often trade on so-called pink sheets rather than with continuous quotes on major exchanges. Dishonest brokers can buy the microcaps at issue in bulk, hype them into visibility, then sell from their inventory.

> Microcaps are the place to be for manipulators and those who allow themselves to be swayed by stories of incredible riches to be.

The typical story goes something like this: "Smart investors are rushing into X company stock, up 35 percent over the last two days. X company has discovered a deposit of lithium in a (faraway) Asian country. The ore grade is 75 percent lithium, potentially the richest in the world. Big battery makers are knocking down the door. Shares are up 50 percent in two days, and they could quadruple before hitting the multiple of companies with mines half as rich...." This is a play on greed and foolishness. It is true that North America was once a faraway place with unknown resources. Napoleon underpriced the Louisiana Purchase at US$12 million, which was cheap even in the early nineteenth century. He needed cash and the U.S. wanted more land. Let's say that such deals don't happen too often. They are developing industries in developing markets. The risks are huge. Of course, if one risk turns out to be a bonanza, a lot of flops will be recovered. But the odds remain very long against it.

Investors continue to be tantalized by stories of riches to be, but groupthink, fed by dishonest stock brokers, continues to flourish in the American pink sheet market of microcap stocks and in Canadian venture exchange stocks. Microcaps are the place to be for manipulators and those who allow themselves to be swayed by stories of incredible riches to be. It is true that both Apple Inc. and Microsoft Corp. were once small stocks, but for every microcap that becomes an Apple, there are hundreds that absorb money and die.

Avoiding the pitfalls of mob-chased microcaps is easy. Don't buy them. The virtue of large- and mid-cap stocks followed by analysts, owned by large investment funds and pension funds, and often reviewed by the financial press is the visibility of the company and the many number crunchers who review their documents and operations. Requirements to file annual reports with regulators add to the difficulty of running these companies as sluices for the money of innocents. That it has happened is certain, but it remains true that the bigger the company, the larger the capitalization, and the more well-known it is, the tougher it is for crooks to inflate a bubble. Size is a partial antidote for groupthink. As for the biggest of all in Canadian terms, Nortel Networks, it was an inside job, its decline driven by wretched accounting.

GROUP ANALYSIS AND PRIVATE ANALYSIS

If you go with the group, then you need to have a fine sense of timing of when to get in and when to get out. The higher a stock's valuation, the more critical it is to sense a peak and then to leave. On the other hand, if you reject what a group does and just buy for the long run or because a stock is too cheap for its underlying prospects, timing is less important.

During the dot-com frenzy of the late 1990s, trusted bank stocks were sold off. Royal Bank common stock fell from $21 at the beginning of 1998 to $15 at the beginning of 2000. Investors were selling real gold to buy what turned out to be mostly fool's gold. Pencil work to estimate dividends and total returns in Royal Bank yielded to the mass market belief that companies with no earnings, sometimes no sales, sometimes no plan, would soar. Hopes crashed.

In the end, groupthink is like rocket fuel. It makes things go up, and when it is gone and momentum is lost, the rocket crashes. Overpaying to get into a play that has already been run is foolish. Selling out when the worst is over and a rebound is possible is also foolish. The crowd is the greater fool. It is the individual making his or her informed decisions about how an asset matches criteria for multiples of price to earnings, price to sales, dividends, dividend growth, and so on who has the edge in the long run.

ETHICAL INVESTING

We cannot avoid a detour into a special category of group thinking. Ethical investing is a process of excluding assets such as stocks and bonds issued by companies that offend the beliefs or wishes of certain investors. Examples are sin stocks such as shares of companies that make and sell liquor, wine, beer, guns, military aircraft, pornography, fast food, products related to contraception or abortion, and gambling, or use animals to test some products. Other activists object to companies that do not have satisfactory controls on pollution, trade with countries activists would prefer they not, have civil rights records offensive to some persons, or do not accord sufficient rights to women and persons of varied sexual identities.

> It is almost impossible to exclude every company doing something that someone would object to and still have a portfolio.

During the dot-com mania of the late 1990s, ethical funds did relatively well in comparison to old economy funds. Ethical funds usually did not object to software companies like Microsoft Corp. and Apple Inc. Those were hot stocks, while old economy stocks like beer and wine just limped along.

As a general principle, when the choices of investments are reduced, portfolio risk tends to rise and returns tend to fall. Further, as Patrick McKeough, publisher of *The Successful Investor* and other market advisory letters, has noted, "It is acceptable to use any standards you like to pick stocks. But when you pick an advisor on the basis that he or she shares your prejudices, you are reducing your potential gains."

There is also a problem of ethical integration. A chartered bank may be quite neutral in its ethical practices and so not offend some ethical investors. But it may do business with a weapons maker or perhaps just cash a dividend cheque or a paycheque from a liquor maker. We don't suggest investors be blind to genocide or companies that peddle narcotics it knows will fall into the hands of street drug dealers. But we do think that it is almost impossible to exclude every company doing something that someone would object to and still have a portfolio.

Moreover, if you buy broad market index funds, you have to accept some ethical taints. Finally, an ethical index — and they do exist — replicated in an investment fund merely combines the selection problem with a fee for winnowing out companies that might be good investments. Bottom line: By all means you should exclude what is genuinely offensive, but don't carry the battle to the next level of companies that do business with the objectionable companies. Or to the next level of companies that do business with companies that do business with the objectionable companies. It cannot work.

CHAPTER 2

Leverage: Using Others' Money to Make Your Own

Borrowing to invest is ancient in concept and practice. It was done in Babylon in 1,600 BCE with the understanding and promise that if the borrower did not repay what was owed, they'd suffer the ultimate devaluation — death. The rules have gotten more lenient, but the ways of borrowing range from banks to brothers-in-law, from mortgage investment corporations that specialize in property loans to pawn shops that are much the same in the sense of lending on the security of property. Money loaned must be repaid with interest on agreed terms, and if the loan is not repaid, the consequences will have to be faced. The borrower's property may be taken in a loan secured by his or her house, perhaps a car will be repossessed, or in the case of stock financed with a loan from a stock broker, the stock will be sold off until the loan is satisfied. In finance, no matter how modern, the idea of security is never really far from a pawn.

Borrowing money has been one of the cornerstones of commerce. From the thirteenth century, when Venetian merchants travelled to various ports of call to trade goods, debt has always been a way to facilitate transactions. It was intended to bridge the time between making something or delivering it and payment for the goods. From the farmer buying seeds, feed, and fertilizer on credit and paying off the loan once the harvest is sold to the shop owner paying for goods thirty days after they have been delivered, credit oils the wheels of commerce.

For many, debt is seen as a modern phenomenon. It isn't, for the linkage of amount borrowed with time of payment on specified terms is documented in *A History of Interest Rates* by Sidney Homer and Richard Sylla.[1] Credit has been with us since the advent of commerce.

> In finance, no matter how modern, the idea of security is never really far from a pawn.

GOOD DEBT AND BAD DEBT

Borrowing to invest is often referred to as leverage. Just like a lever moving on its fulcrum, you can increase the power and reach of the financial transaction. The interest rate charged is larger than the cost of the loan (money borrowed from a bank or through a bond on better terms) and thus leaves the lending financial company better off after making the transactions. Even thirty-day credit on an invoice is a form of leverage, for one can make a tidy living on sums held for a month before payment.

The implication for investors is that while the cost of a loan with a longer amortization may be more palatable, it does come at quite a high cost of interest. So, while the nominal interest rate of a loan may be appealing, the length of the term of the loan is where the cost and profit lie. A long loan at a lower interest rate makes sense for the lender as long as its cost of borrowing is less than the rate at which it lends. If you wonder how no-interest car loans work, worry not. The manufacturer or the captive importer owned by the manufacturer moves the debt owed by the consumer up its cost structure and builds it into the price of the car. If you juice up the deal by paying cash, there is often a discount on the finance charge built into the supposedly interest-free loan.

Most businesses use leverage. Warren Buffett's most successful investment has been his insurance operation. Insurance is a form of leverage. The insurer receives periodic payments as premiums and pays out large sums should a described calamity come to pass. As the insurance company's operations grow, and if its underwriting of risk is competent, its insurance premiums will exceed what it pays out in claims. In Mr. Buffett's case, the insurance operations have allowed him to invest other people's money and to reap the rewards by keeping payouts below premiums charged.

The way you leverage and what you do with the borrowed funds is key. Let's review some basic principles to see how to benefit from using leverage. Time, as we'll see, is as important as interest rate.

For a depreciating asset, time works against you. As your outstanding debt decreases, the value of the asset is also decreasing. Sometimes the asset is worth less than the debt you used to purchase the asset. When this upside-down situation occurs, you find yourself in a position of financial servitude. You cannot sell the asset because it is worth less than what the bank loaned you, yet you need to sell the asset as you may not require it or be able to afford it. The only choice is to continue to pay off the loan until you can sell the asset.

INVESTING VERSUS SPECULATING

Benjamin Graham, the classical scholar who invented security analysis, explained that the mistake most investors make is to confuse investing with speculating. Speculating is neither illegal nor immoral and in fact can be quite lucrative. However, the main difference between investing and speculating is that when investing, you have a high probability of seeing your invested capital once again in the future. While the capital may be at risk temporarily if the market goes down for a time, the entirety of its value is not in question. When speculating, you are quite certain that all your investment is at risk of losing much or all of its value.

Many investors will use leverage when investing in real estate or stocks. Borrowing money to invest in stocks is usually done through the opening of a margin account. In fact, margin accounts were one of the financial innovations of the 1920s. These accounts exacerbated the major decline of 1929. For investing in bonds at the very low interest rates prevailing as we write *Cherished Fortune*, borrowing costs are too high. Borrowing to invest in riskier junk bonds can work on paper, but the investor who does this is balancing the risk of the bond's default against his own obligation to pay. It's a lousy bet.

For stocks, it's different. Investors commonly use margin loans issued by the dealer or broker who extends credit based on the value of a stock or portfolio of stocks. Most well-established stocks will enable the speculator or investor to put down 30 percent of the value of the stock and borrow 70 percent of the value. The interest rate charged is usually a markup of the prime rate; for example, prime plus 1 percent.

Let's run through an example: You want to buy your favourite Canadian telecom provider, say BCE Inc., the biggest of all in the industry. It trades for around $60 and pays a dividend of $0.755 per share on a quarterly basis. You determine that this low-volatility staple of the Canadian economy is an ideal candidate for borrowing to invest. The fact that dividends have a history of growing over time is also a plus. However, you have identified that, as a telecom provider, the company has a large amount of debt backed by its large network. Nevertheless, it is a solid stock in a stable and insulated business that pays a nice dividend.

> When investing, you have a high probability of seeing your invested capital again. When speculating, your investment is at risk of losing all its value.

You decide that you will invest $60,000 and thus purchase 1,090 shares at the recent price of $55. You also know that the stated dividend will return $3.02 per share per year, which for 1,090 shares works out to $3,292 per year. Some aggressive investors might be tempted to borrow the full 70 percent of the purchase price, thus borrowing $42,000 and only putting down the balance of $18,000.

You plan on sleeping every night and you have studied the stock's history. It is not immune from events in the wider market. Back in 2008, BCE shares fell from $41 to $24, a 40 percent drop. A sound stock for sure, but BCE carries market risk.

What could go wrong? The obvious is that a company-specific event or a market dislocation could cause the stock to fall. In the case of an unleveraged investor, not much happens, except for some stomach-churning worry. For the leveraged investor, you can also add additional financial considerations like a margin call. That call happens when the value of the stock falls below minimum loan requirements. In this case, the requirements are equity of 30 percent of the original investment.

In effect, the broker will loan you $42 for each $60 share you purchase. But if the stock falls below the margin, which is the money the broker loaned, 70 percent of $60, would be at risk. The broker would sell sufficient stock to restore the 70/30 loan ratio. You would lose half the dividend income and half the stock.

Introducing leverage to this type of speculating endeavour can be a hazard to your financial health. Losing your hard-earned money is unpleasant, to say the least. But it can happen even with the most mundane of assets if you borrow so much that a small downturn in the market or exchange value of the stock becomes a big hit on your net worth.

TIME

The concept of time is often lost on investors. As in most sports competition with a set amount of time and two opponents competing, the management of the "clock" can become an important tool for victory. In leveraged investing with borrowed money, the clock runs against you. Buying and holding with borrowed money reduces the margin of profit and increases risk.

The profit from the investment is based on being able to sell the asset at a higher price than your purchase price. However, this date cannot be too far off because each month the cost of carrying the investment chips away at your bank account and your future expected profit.

Speculators — that is, traders who hope for a fast profit on what may be borrowed money rather than buying the stock outright and holding it for many years, even through several business cycles — can find themselves in this time squeeze. If the asset price is falling, you need to fill the cash gap in order to stop the bleeding, and the longer the bleeding lasts, the more it will eat into your profits, then your capital, then even into assets outside of your investment. Your home could be at stake.

LAWYERS AND DEALS

We need to make a very important point about taking on debt to make investments. That is the variability of legal risk. You can be sure that commercial lenders such as banks, credit unions, retail stores, and issuers of universal plastic, such as banks that issue MasterCard or other cards, have taken time to ensure that they get paid. The remedies spelled out in the microprint agreements are clear. Payday lenders also have well-engineered debt agreements. You enter into these agreements at your risk and violate them at potentially great expense.

Where the small print ends, law begins. If you borrow money, as opposed to being a partner or coventurer who owns a business or asset the money will finance, you have to pay it back. This is so simple it seems not to require mention. However, when the lender is also a principal who joins in the management of whatever the money is for, things get less clear.

The point of this is that one should read, take legal advice, and know the lender's recourse if the loan is not paid. This, too, seems too simple to require mention, but a friendly "here, sign this" offer can be a trip into financial slavery. You have a technical exposure when you use plastic to buy something at the drug store, but for the few bucks you owe, it's not a big deal. If you leverage a business on a large loan, it is a big deal. Anyone who takes on an obligation without getting it checked by a lawyer, preferably a specialist in the kind of deal involved, is pennywise and pound foolish. It is bad business and a huge potential risk to your fortune.

TAX SHIELD

Borrowing costs for investment in income-producing assets are usually tax deductible, provided that the loan is not used for contributions to a registered retirement savings plan, a tax-free savings account, or a registered education savings plan; to pay late income tax installments or payments; or for a loan for a car for strictly personal use or other non-business expenses. In other words, any investment in which an expectation of taxable income is present can have its interest charges deducted against the income earned. If the asset to be acquired is, for example, raw land with no prospect of rental or other use, any interest paid on a loan to buy the land will not be deductible from income. After all, it produces no income. If money is borrowed to improve the land, perhaps by adding drainage or fencing, the interest expense can be added to the asset's cost. If in future the land is sold, the adjusted cost base, enhanced with the interest and other cost of improvements, would be higher and any taxable capital gain, therefore, lower. In this case, the cost deduction for interest paid is deferred but not eliminated.

There is a way to make interest deductible. It is called the Smith Manoeuvre, after British Columbia financial strategist Fraser Smith, who is given credit for inventing it. The technique turns the mortgage on your principal residence, which is not tax deductible, into a cost stream that is deductible.

For those who have the ability to obtain a mortgage that can be extended to a home equity line of credit connected to a conventional mortgage, the transaction is easy. As you pay off your mortgage every month, the home's equity value increases. That in turn allows you to increase the outstanding balance on your line of credit. The line of credit is used to buy income-producing assets like stocks.

The procedure is actually a simple concept. Sell existing financial assets to raise cash to pay off your mortgage. Then get a line of credit secured by your home. Use the line of credit to buy back what you sold to pay the mortgage or to buy other investment assets. Interest on the line of credit used to buy income-producing assets is deductible. Any profit from the deal can be used to pay down the line of credit, for it was used to get money to invest for hopefully taxable results.

For those who use the Smith Manoeuvre, there is risk that the line of credit cost will rise. In fact, you may have invested in a portfolio that is also interest-rate sensitive, thereby decreasing its value if and when interest rates rise at the very same time that interest charges on the line of credit are rising. You could be pushed into the red. However, the end result of the plan should ideally be that you shave years from your mortgage amortization while building up an investment portfolio. Of course, the transaction of selling stocks to raise cash to pay down the mortgage may generate capital gains that are taxable. There may be other transactions costs, such as brokerage fees. In the end, the Smith Manoeuvre can increase risk and expose the investor to an interest rate squeeze if the cost of borrowing rises. But it is an example of leverage that, if wisely used, can add to one's wealth. The plan assumes that you will be an active portfolio manager and will control risk and manage your tax liabilities actively. It is not a free ride or necessarily an easy one. Properly done, it is a way to convert what could be thousands of dollars of mortgage interest, though not mortgage principal payback, to a deductible cost.

> A crisis is an opportunity to buy for the investor who has cash and courage to act.

TIMING

With leverage, timing is vital. When you invest in a portfolio, quality stock, or other sound asset, its quality will shine through over time. The more time passes, the less each up- and down-market move will matter. Your growing equity will reduce the risk that your loan will be called for payment by the lender or that you will be forced to sell some of the asset in a margin call demand.

A crisis is an opportunity to buy for the investor who has cash and courage to act. A crisis brings a buyers' strike, which makes prices fall. Those with the capital and the intestinal fortitude can do quite well.

How should you pick your spots for leverage? There are two critical variables. The first is the economic cycle, for markets have seasons. The second criterion is your own wealth and obligations. You do not necessarily want to be adding leverage three years from retirement, for example. In short, the asset prices that attract you have to merit being aggressive. As well, you have to be in a position to weather unpredicted storms.

GOOD DEALS AND BAD DEALS

It is essential to match the time you borrow with the time you think it will take for your leveraged investment to bloom into the value you expect. Were you running a store and buying inventory on credit, you would want to match the sale date or period of the products you order with what it will cost you to buy them.

If the cost of the products is, say, $100 each and you borrow what amounts to $30 for each product, including interest on a loan due at a definite date after expected sale of the products, you have to get $130 or you will lose money. If there is not enough profit on each round to cover costs and provide a margin for effort and risk, the chances are strong that you will eventually go out of business.

> Even government bonds have potential for loss if inflation reduces their market value or rising interest rates drive down their value before maturity.

A loan with a definite date is a term loan. The fixed rate of interest allows you to estimate full cost. A reasonable loan margin is $30. This is a tidy deal.

Now consider how you could finance the order. If you have a callable demand loan with a floating rate, you do not know what it will cost or how long you have the money. It looks like a death sentence for your money, yet many investors take these deals.

Technically, a margin loan from your investment dealer is a demand loan, though the conditions of the deal are spelled out in advance. The trigger will be a slump in the stock price. The interest rates may change, but probably not too quickly. If the variable rate demand loan is for a stock you expect to rise X percent in a defined period, the margin loan could be considered reasonable. But not all loans are so neat, and many are much riskier.

Let's say that you acquire a home equity line of credit (HELOC), securing the loan against the equity in your home. The loan will have a floating rate, or you could extend your mortgage and get a fixed rate. The risk is that the asset you buy, if it takes a large part of your equity, could result in loss of home. A HELOC is a way of extracting money from houses or condos that have appreciated greatly, as many have. In the U.S., a HELOC in default can result in loss of the pledged collateral; that is, your home. In Canada, HELOCs are recourse loans; that is, the lender can both seize and sell the home and then sue the borrower for any deficiency.

The risk of these deals is apparent. Depending on the amount of leverage, you are risking loss of home for an uncertain profit in an investment that may be speculative. And do not doubt that any investment can be speculative. Even government bonds have potential for loss if, over time, inflation reduces their market value or, more to the point, rising interest rates drive down the value of the bonds before maturity. Moreover, a small position, say $10,000, in a solid bank stock whose drop by, say, 50 percent would be of little consequence in a $500,000 portfolio would be of great importance were the shares to drop by $300,000 in a $500,000 portfolio.

REVERSE MORTGAGES

Home prices have soared in many areas of Canada and, for that matter, other countries in recent years. People who have owned their homes for decades often have huge appreciation. It may seem useful to tap it to buy a new car, to pay for trips to lovely places, or to make investments. Conventional loans can be secured on your property to qualify for low single-digit interest rates. Special loans with no intermediate payments can be done. They are reverse mortgages, and they are seldom a good idea. Only for people with no other sources of funds and in desperate need of cash, often people with poor credit ratings, is a reverse mortgage appropriate. First, a few words of explanation.

Reverse mortgages are ordinary mortgages running backwards. They are usually made to persons age fifty-five and over, often sixty-five and over depending on the lender, and for not more than 65 percent of the appraised value of a home. In Canada, the Canadian Home Income Plan (CHIP), offered by HomEquity Bank, which is the main reverse mortgage lender in the country, assesses a home and makes a loan against it. There are no payments, and all the money paid out is considered a return of capital with no tax. Sounds good, but understand that interest is charged at higher than conventional mortgage rates and compounds against the value of the home. If the reverse mortgage is paid off before an anticipated event, such as the sale of the house, there may be penalties levied against the borrower. There may be appraisal fees and closing fees, and there certainly should be legal fees, for you *must* run the deal by a lawyer who knows contracts and real estate law. It is difficult to discern the true interest rates with the plethora of add-on fees. The difficulty of determining the cost of lending fees is itself a red flag these days. In spite of the famous personalities who peddle these products on television — who probably do not need to borrow via reverse mortgages — the best advice is to stay away.

In spite of the famous personalities who peddle these products on television, the best advice is to stay away from reverse mortgages.

The concept of a reverse mortgage is re-amortizing; that is, extracting some equity from a home. If you have owned your home for many years, a HELOC will make more sense, for the interest rate will be lower, there will be no compounding, and early payoff will be easy. HELOCs can be structured to require just interest payments. You do have to service these loans, but the lending banks will be upfront and ready to disclose fees. Moreover, if your relationship with the bank is good and you have a bit of mortgage left to pay, it is all the easier to get a HELOC going.

A very special word of caution is in order. Some people are lured into or tempted by deals in which, say the promoters, they can convert dead money in a home into a live and promising investment. As the deals we have seen in confess-and-cry columns in many publications have attested, the concept of taking a solid and low-risk investment in one's home and putting it at risk in what are often dangerous, ill-advised, and even rip-off schemes is foolish, even idiotic. There are many stories of elderly people who attend so-called investor meetings, then pony up cash they get from reverse mortgages, then after one or two payments from the scheme get nothing.

The risk profile of someone who would impair a good asset for financial garbage is, of course, not that of an experienced investor. As a means of making money, even if the proposed scheme works, it is bad risk management. Our advice for reverse mortgage–based investments is 1) talk to your accountant; 2) see a financial planner who is fee-based (that is, sells nothing but his or her time); 3) research the proposed deal and check with your provincial or territorial securities commission; and 4) talk to a lawyer if you are intent on doing the deal. The few cases in which a reverse mortgage is okay are when home owners have absolutely no other resources. They must have a desperate need for cash. The shorter the loan period, the less interest will be due, for interest compounds in reverse mortgages. If not repaid, then the death of the borrower and sale of the house will eventually generate cash to clear the debt. To make any sense of a reverse mortgage, use of the money must be for life today, not investments at risk. In other words, if you have nothing else, check out the reverse mortgage. That is the only time it can be a suitable plan. Remember, if you do go into the deal, time is working against you. It is really a poor position to be in. If you are still interested, visit this Government of Canada website: canada.ca/en/financial-consumer-agency/services/mortgages.html.

LENDERS' REMEDIES

Institutions granting loans have their paperwork written by lawyers who know their stuff. Not only should one read the loan contracts, but, for significant sums, the borrower should have the paperwork reviewed by a lawyer familiar with lending and this branch of contract law. The boilerplate wording may not be changeable, but the arithmetic, the numbers — interest rate, when due, late penalties, et cetera — are often variable.

Risks rise with sums borrowed. Thus, a dicey loan for $10,000 when you have $1 million in cash and negotiable bonds can be paid with a cheque. But a $100,000 loan when you have half a million, $400,000 of which is in your house, is a different risk.

Not all loan contracts are equal. Banks lend at published rates on terms anyone can read. On the other extreme, payday loan stores have a superficially reasonable loan rate and then add on fees that can make some loans have three-figure interest rates. There are records of loans with short-term fees and related charges that make the annual loan rates equal 1,200 percent. That is scandalous, but the same process of piling on charges goes for pawn shops, many of which charge interest below the usury limits, often 30 percent per year, and then add storage charges and appraisal fees, handling fees, and documentation fees that push total interest charges into three figures.

Finally, we should mention balloon payments that are often part of consumer and even business loans. A balloon payment is a final installment to end a loan that may be many times previous payments. They are common in U.S. mortgages where not all the loan is paid off or amortized as the end of the payments approach. Technically, the obligation to return capital when a bond comes to the end of its term is a balloon payment. Car loans also can have balloon payments.

> The worst damage in the mortgage crisis happened to people who did not read their mortgage agreements.

Balloon payments are not troublesome if you know they are coming and have to be paid. They are dangerous for borrowers who have not read their loan agreements. U.S. data obtained during the 2008–2009 mortgage crisis showed that the key indicator of whether a borrower would lose their house was whether they had read their mortgage. The mortgage crisis was compounded with fraudulent acts by many lenders, but the worst damage happened to people who did not read their mortgage agreements and run them by their own lawyers.[2]

The safest loans from the point of view of the borrower are those for a fixed and known rate of interest for a fixed and known time. The least safe are floating rate demand loans. It follows that risk is best managed with the former and that the latter loan format exposes any speculative investment, which all stocks and most bonds are, to additional risk. Moreover, when an asset that is illiquid, such as real estate, is financed with a floating rate demand loan, the borrower has put themselves at serious risk of default. If the lender demands return of money in a tough market, the borrower could have to sell collateral, even their house, to satisfy the demand. A bad deal for sure. This is the classic interest rate squeeze, which we'll delve into in discussing real estate investment.

MANAGING LEVERAGE

Human nature being what it is, success in investing, like in any endeavour, can bring a sense of invincibility. In the business, we call it hubris. Hubris has taken down many investors at some point or another. The good ones do not repeat that mistake. The bad investors never recover from the mistake.

Winning a bet or taking a stock profit is like an elixir. Winning with leverage is even more intoxicating. If you are fortunate enough to find yourself in the lead using leverage, remember that it cuts both ways. It magnifies the results of your investment decisions and can in fact turn a winning situation into a losing one in a hurry.

Determining when to leverage is an endless hunt. Find an asset that seems a good investment. If you can get it at a discount when the market is down, you have a margin of safety. The next step is to finance the transaction in such a way that the asset being purchased is largely financing the deal. In a few cases, the purchase of the asset will finance itself with no requirement of capital.

> If you are fortunate enough to find yourself in the lead using leverage, remember that a winning situation can turn into a losing one in a hurry.

If you buy a rental building, the cash flow generated from the asset services the debt. While you own the asset, the tenants, customers, or renters of your asset will, hopefully, reduce the outstanding debt. This assumes, of course, that the rental income flow is sufficient to cover the costs. But it does not always work out. The less equity you have, the more this strategy can backfire. A lender will have to accept the terms, including interest rate risk, the risk that you will not manage the asset well, the risk that interest rates will stay within expected boundaries, and even the risk that adjacent properties will not become nuisances that reduce the value of the property against which they are lending funds and impair the value of their security. This is a lot of risk. For a few years, the main risk is occupancy and interest rate moves. Management skill and the term of the loan cover those risks. Over a period of thirty years, a lot more can happen. Leverage risk seldom totally dissipates.

Individual investors cannot afford to hold more than a handful of rental properties. The costs of finance and management make it nearly impossible for a single person to assemble scores of properties across the country in various niches of the property market.

There is a different approach to risk: that's putting your money into companies with high cash flow, such as alcoholic beverage makers and companies that package food and personal care products. All of these companies have low input costs and high product prices. This is leveraging debt on sales and profit. Consider soap and personal care product manufacturer and marketer Procter & Gamble Company. It has been able to make acquisitions through a history that dates back to 1837. By purchasing assets and financing these purchases by debt, the company grows its sales and income. Operationally, these new product lines fit into the distribution network and even existing manufacturing capabilities. The associated debt is then reduced as this new business is integrated and its profits directed to retiring the debt. After a decade, or even half a decade, the company experiences a growth in sales and profits, all the while seeing the value of the equity of the business increase as well.

Investors can also use asset leverage with split shares. They are created with a portfolio of dividend-paying stocks. One group of shareholders, the preferred holders, gets all the dividends and the other, the common holders, gets all the capital gains exposure. Investment bankers create these structures and take handsome commissions for their work. If you want this kind of leveraged investment, choose the capital shares or the income shares. Do not pick both. If you do, you are paying a fee to hold what the plain shares would provide. The fees, in fact, just finance the unbundling and then repackaging of the two types of returns. The security for the preferred shareholder is that there is twice as much equity as he or she owns and thus twice the dividend. For the common shareholder, the leverage comes from the fact that the appreciation will be doubled. One part of the asset levers the other. Of course, the common shareholders give up the protection of dividend flow as a cushion for falling prices, and the dividend shareholders give up capital appreciation and the companion risk of capital depreciation.

New issues of stock can also have their own built-in sales leverage. Consider installment receipts, which are used as an inducement for initial public offerings, or IPOs. Investors sign up to pay and receive shares in pieces. Thus, a share will begin to trade for $10 per share, but the amount due on closing is a portion, usually half of this IPO share value. The balance is due usually in twelve or eighteen months for this period, and positive appreciation is magnified. In this case, the shareholder is using the money of the corporation for the time period for his or her own benefit.

In the case of installment receipts, adverse corporate results or industry headwinds could see the value of the equity erode just as the second installment is due. As a shareholder, you are forced to either sell at an inopportune time or pony up the balance of the payment. This is time leverage and it is precarious.

CROWDFUNDING

There are creative ways of obtaining loans for investments. These methods go far beyond asking for a loan from your friendly bank or credit union. Rather, they are at the edge of commercial lending and in some cases beyond it.

Crowdfunding has gotten to be a fairly common alternative to going to a formal lender. Web-based services match up potential lenders and borrowers. The idea is to enable peer-to-peer lending, P2P for short. It has gained a great deal of traction in the United Kingdom, where ventures such as music albums by new groups are likely to be given a thumbs down by traditional lenders. P2P-enabling sites may take a fee or a small cut of business for their costs. It is, nevertheless, democratic, efficient, and as secure as the parties who meet up on these financial dating services care to make their deals. For a small business, P2P has much to offer, including low costs, tailor-made loan conditions, acceptable repayment options, and recourse for non-payment that might include physical delivery of whatever goods or services the deals involve.[3] As a form of investment, we'd offer caution. A P2P deal that is a partnership could bloom into a fortune. If the deal is merely a loan with a payment schedule, even if the interest charged is generous, it's risky or troublesome, as the case may be.

MEZZANINE LENDING

Going up the scale of loan risk, there is mezzanine lending. The word "mezzanine" refers to the concept of a level between the ground floor of straight bank loan with interest and the upper level of pure stock investment and risk. Mezzanine lenders typically structure deals with hefty interest and some equity participation. They provide cash when a straight interest loan, even one secured by the borrower's house or other assets, won't be sufficient and a business is too young to support a stock sale.

An individual investor can, however, structure a loan in mezzanine style with some interest at a rate that reflects the risks of an early stage investment and some equity participation if it works out. Early stage investment in tech sector and internet ideas are often mezzanine loans.

UNIVERSAL LIFE INSURANCE

One of the more creative concepts of debt leverage is borrowing to buy universal life policies. A universal life policy is one in which the portion of the policy that generates cash value is invested in stocks or bonds. The idea is that the slow cash value accumulation of ordinary whole life policies is replaced or enhanced by whatever investments in stocks or bonds the person who buys the policy, usually the insured person, may choose.

Good concept, but it has lots of pitfalls. Universal life policies are complex, difficult to understand, and often heavy with fees. The sales people can get upfront commissions of as much as 160 percent of the first-year premium. Regulators have tried to reduce these incentives, which even go as far as paying people to sign up for these policies, but huge commissions are part of the problem.

These days, there is a new twist to universal life policy risk. Major insurance companies have captive banks that essentially lend only in connection with the insurance sold. So, a person buys life insurance with a loan of as much as 100 percent of premiums due, gets a universal life policy that can be invested in the company's mutual funds with life

insurance protections such as immunity from ordinary lawsuits for collection of loans in default, then uses the policy as collateral for yet more
loans. The leverage of these deals can be astonishing. If you borrow
$10,000 for a premium and then sign up for a venture with far more risk,
you are at the end of the line with a lot of risk that may not be well defined
or well understood. This can be a way to build a portfolio with coverage
for the event of early death, but it is also incredibly risky.

Many universal life policies allow the owner of the policy to take a loan against the policy. The insurance company or its captive lender may have financed the premiums. In theory, growing cash value should reduce the value of the outstanding loan, the sums to be paid upon death of the insured, or both. The insurance company itself may be charging interest on any loan within the policy that enables purchase of assets, typically but not necessarily various index funds.

> Given the complexity of universal life policies and the difficulty of understanding your position, life is simpler without these tortuous, complex deals.

The policies tend not to require repayment of principal. Whatever
interest is not paid to the insurance company can be deducted from
the cash value of the policy. Cash taken out of a universal life policy
will tend to reduce its value as insurance. But red caution flags have
to be raised, for the policy becomes a murky pot of risks in which a
portfolio investment used as life insurance is compromised by investments and the entire deal is laden with commissions for the various
cooks stirring the pot.[4]

Most of all, given the complexity of universal life policies and
the difficulty of understanding the position of a borrower/insured/
investor, we'd suggest that life is simpler without these tortuous deals.
As a means of running a portfolio of stocks backed by complex life
insurance investments, we'd compare this to a kind of Russian roulette.
Most of the time, a properly structured loan from a captive company to
buy a universal life policy with one's choice of stocks or bonds should
work. But if the assets purchased collapse, the policy will be worth less.
The loan to pay premiums to the captive bank is still outstanding. The

only way out may be via the fundamental concept of life insurance — the death of the insured — or some elaborate refinancing plans. We think that captive lender universal life policies represent risks one should not take.

ASSET-BASED LENDING

A small business can finance some of its operations by borrowing against its receivables. The receivable goods secure the loan. A special kind of this lending or, from the other side, borrowing, is commercial factoring, often done just as a discount on bills that have already been sent out. The business borrowing through this delays payment of bills. It is a form of do-it-yourself factoring.[5]

An asset-based loan, like any other loan taken by a business, can be converted to a credit that the business owner can use for investment through the business. If the asset is at risk, as any stock is, then it adds to the general risk of the business. If the asset is a low-risk device such as a government bond, then it may reduce general business risk. However, government bonds in general pay less interest than commercial factors will charge. So this manipulation, even if legal, would be a money loser. If the asset purchased with the factor loan is used in the business to add to its sales or profits, then it makes sense.

LEVERAGE AND TIME

Leverage and debt are part of commerce and finance. The most important factor that will determine success in using debt and leverage is time. A short-term loan used to buy a stock that rises smartly and is then sold, with the profits used to pay the loan off, has served its purpose. But if the quick flip turns into a long-term hold, paying interest for months or years may devastate the investment. Clearly, adding leverage to an investment adds to the management issue and makes passive buy-and-hold investing more difficult. However, if you find yourself on the opposite end of leverage, just like the polar bear, it will maul you in an instant. You wind up in the unenviable and potentially devastating position of someone who owes more money than is coming in through dividends or interest to pay the loan. It's generating red ink, and there is no easy way out. You may be tempted to short the stock, thus making money if it should fall further. But mere oscillation of price may stick you with two costs: margin interest and interest to borrow the stock you have sold short.

Thus, leverage should be used only with great care. Inevitably, it increases risk if things do not work out as expected. The inventory the small shop owner buys on credit may not sell well, and even if it does produce the expected profit, some of the gain will have to be shared with the lender in the form of interest. So leverage always changes the risk-to-reward ratio. There are no free rides in business or investing.

Adding leverage to an investment adds to the management issue and makes passive buy-and-hold investing more difficult.

CHAPTER 3

Valuation: What It's Worth

Valuation is a big word and a big concept. What a stock or any other asset is worth is part pencil work and part instinct or, much the same thing, familiarity with the asset. Knowing the worth of a potential investment or one you have and are considering selling is key to winning the game. Even critical to staying in the game.

The idea of finding core value is, in a sense, avoidance of error. If a stock or other asset has abundant available data such as earnings trends, earnings per share, book value of the company, book value per share, sales trends, return on cost, return on equity, and so on — the list of variables that can be shaken out of published financial statements — then the problem of calculating value is pencil work and comparison with like companies. If it's a mutual fund or exchange traded fund, there are abundant data available on the manager's website.

The less data that are available, the harder it is to make firm calculations of value. Take out earnings if the company has none, and all that is left is the balance sheet of assets and liabilities. If the assets are intellectual property and goodwill, the guessing gets harder. If the company is young and has no sales yet, which was the case for many dot-coms in 1998, the guessing is mostly crystal ball work. And if analysts give thumbs up to companies that burn up capital on the assumption that eating capital rather than creating it is smart, which was a value measure in the dot-com frenzy, calculations are the stuff of witches and cauldrons. You will have better odds shooting craps.

We'll assume that there are enough solid variables to set values on the stock or bond in question. If you know the value of an asset and the market price is a good deal less, then you can buy and hold or sell for a quick profit. If the price exceeds the value on paper, the premium is a bet on the future value of the asset. The essence of wise investing is sorting out underlying value, which is seldom the exact market price, and the market's premium or — it happens — deduction for a stock with a crummy outlook. For bonds that are rated, the websites of Standard & Poors, Fitch, DBRS, and Moody's Investor Services are great allies. They cannot judge a price, but they can distill the value in bonds, from sound government issues to sheer junk nearing the edge of the cliff of default.

> The essence of wise investing is sorting out underlying value, which is seldom the market price.

Mispricing does happen, for markets are subject to delirious highs, as they were in the extraordinary rise of the dot-coms from 1998 to 2000, and as they have recently been in the ascent — and frequent descent, in days, to double-digit percentage losses — of blockchain currencies like Bitcoin and, of course, marijuana stocks, which have a delirium of their own. Mispricing also occurs on the way down, as in the years following the dot-com bust and, of course, the meltdown of the vast and unsound U.S. mortgage market in 2008. "Market prices are seldom the right prices," said a research chief of a major brokerage who was later head of one of the biggest investment banks in Canada.

If you distill the underlying or fundamental value from the wobbles of the market, you can make wise choices to buy when the asset is underpriced and sell when it is hopelessly overpriced. Skilled valuation is the essence of shrewd investing, for it makes tangible the concept of buying cheap and selling dear. Developing a sense of what beckons for investment and what should be shunned is a matter of book knowledge and market experience.

That is not the end of the story, of course, for markets can take quite a while to settle on accurate value. In the short term, the process of fundamental value and market value converging is chaotic, but in the long run, it works. Buggy whip makers are largely out of business, after all.

The investor's problem is to sort out what is fundamental and what is fluff. Moreover, because the many numbers that make up financial statements are often interrelated (or covariant, in statistical terms), it is essential to pick the numbers that matter and to forget those that either don't count for much or are already included in the important numbers.

The problem for analyzing the value of shares is that most of the companies on stock exchanges, most that issue bonds, and virtually all mutual funds and exchange traded funds are made up of many parts. Valuation requires a strategy or a methodology. It may take time and even induce a few headaches, but — think! — why throw your money into a business or concept unless you understand it? Just as your own business could not exist if you overpaid for goods and services and sold them for less than their value, investment portfolio management requires knowing basic worth.

VALUATION: THE TOOLS

The problem of valuation is deep and complex, for not all investors will agree on a certain value and, of course, you may get your calculations wrong. Insiders in an industry or a company have a sense of what is right, but outsiders, as most investors are, have to use a lot of analytical tools to see what is inside the box. Much analysis is available online, but there is no substitute for pencil and paper work to get a feel quite literally for what makes a company tick. Remember, when you buy financial assets such as stocks, you are investing in somebody else's business. They know a lot about the business. You don't. The bridge to understanding is research. It can be enlightening, and it can help you find bargains and avoid the grief of large losses.

The first step in this process of outsiders getting to have insiders' knowledge is to learn as much as possible from published sources about the industry, the management of a company, the trend of sales and earnings, costs, what professional analysts say, what customers seem to say, and the trend of the industry.

Much of this information is accessible on the internet. Major financial rating agencies such as Standard & Poor's and DBRS (formerly the Dominion Bond Rating Service) make many of their analytical reports publicly available without charge. A visit to Google inevitably produces a flood of opinions. When all of this outsiders' information is assembled, it usually amounts to statistical noise. What the outsider needs is the insider's sense of what is good about the company, what is bad, and, especially where key indicators like earnings per share and book value per share are going. Reading annual reports and quarterly statements, which are available on the websites of public companies, is fundamental. Amazingly, few investors actually do it, preferring to put their money into the hands of managers they have not met who often flaunt their success with statistical nonsense and half-baked theories, taking huge fees whether they succeed or fail, and often buying into businesses that are — as we shall see — utter crap.

Accounting, it has been said, is not unlike watching paint dry. However, it is the most important tool that the investor has in doing their own homework on any company. Analyses of companies are available in quarterly reports and in annual statements along with management guidance, and, for many large companies, there are assessments from brokerage stock analysts. However, reliance on analysts alone is unwise, for their collective record shows groupthink and refusal to face facts. As mentioned in Chapter 2, many analysts who followed Enron (filed for bankruptcy in 2001), Nortel Networks (filed for bankruptcy in 2009), and Bre-X Minerals Ltd. (fraud exposed in 1997, shares became worthless) initially refused to accept increasingly abundant evidence that each was a massive flop.

Crowd mentality led stock analysts to miss the peril of Lehman Brothers, the event that triggered the 2008 financial crisis, because Lehman was an old and eminent firm with valuable business that many analysts sought or whose clients the analysts did not want to shock. Moreover, self-preservation led analysts not to stick their heads out and have them cut off. Staying with majority opinion is safe, though investors who followed the advice of one Wall Street savant, Dick Bove, would have profited handsomely on some of his predictions but lost almost everything after he told his listeners to buy Lehman five weeks before its collapse into worthlessness when it filed for bankruptcy on September 15, 2008.

There is a moral in all this: Do your own analysis. You need not be right to the penny on what a stock may earn. You do not even have to be right at all. The important thing is to avoid the cost of being wrong. Put another way, don't try to beat the market, for you probably won't. Just avoid doing things that are downright stupid.

That is easier than you may think. Avoid overpriced stocks (that is, those with ratios of price to earnings well into two digits, say above thirty); shares of dying companies; shares of incredibly volatile businesses like airlines, which have small profit margins dependent on fuel prices; and new, iffy technologies and products that are either unsettled or that anybody can make.

> Do your own analysis. You need not be right to the penny — the important thing is to avoid the cost of being wrong.

Moreover, the lifespan of many products and companies is getting shorter. In the cell phone business, think of the once great names that have become just background noise: Nokia, which still makes phones; Motorola — good name, big company, not a hot name in phones but solid enough for now; Blackberry — perhaps on the way to becoming a kind of fruit again. In computers, think of Atari for the home and DEC for business mid-range computing. These companies had short and dangerous lives. May the casual investor beware. If there is a rule in all this misery, it is that the more tech-y the firm, the shorter its lifespan may be. There are outliers, of course. Amazon.com Inc. is a tech firm that exists on the web and, of course, in its distribution centres that rival airports in size. But Amazon is first and foremost a retailer. It has the capital to morph into anything else, including cloud computing and perhaps a delivery service propelled by drones. IBM, on the other hand, may call itself a service firm, which is more popular than being a mere hardware maker, but the market is not impressed. It was priced at about US$140 in mid-2018, about where it was in the second half of 2015. In high tech, venerable is not necessarily good.

What is amazing in all this is that many highly paid stock analysts issue buy signals on companies they might more prudently advise be avoided. It all depends on who is doing the valuation.

COLLECTIVE WISDOM: IS THERE SAFETY IN NUMBERS?

Collective thinking led by professional stock analysts and sustained by investors maintained the belief that giant companies with stock on the market worth billions could not be made of lies. Bre-X in particular, discussed in Chapter 2, demonstrates the point.[1]

Perhaps the oddest scam was an attempt by the Saudi Arabian arms merchant and international bon vivant Adnan Khashoggi to sell shares in his plan to find and dig up King Solomon's mines. Shares were to be sold on the old Vancouver Stock Exchange — where else? Khashoggi ran his promotion from his gigayacht, rumoured to cost US$250,000 a day to float and fuel, and whispers from his Canadian arm candy, Anne-Marie Sten, a girl from Woodbridge, Ontario, who wooed (or was wooed by) a string of Eurotrash.[2] Now consider: the Saudi arms hustler and a slinky Canadian woman, and who would not think of this as lavish and great fun to join? Dull pencil pushers who want to keep their fortunes intact. That's who. For the record, even the risk-tolerant VSE thought the King Solomon's mines caper was whimsy carried too far and refused to list it.

The broad category of promotion of dubious ventures is called "putting lipstick on pigs." It is an old sell-side concept in financial markets. In the first years of the millennium, Jack Grubman, then a star analyst at Citigroup investment bank Salomon Smith Barney, hustled many stocks to clients while telling colleagues that the shares were trash. His motives were complex but included getting his tots into a prestigious Manhattan pre-school that was said to be harder to enter than Harvard. The heavyweight in the school was Citigroup — then as now one of the biggest banks in America — head-honcho Sandy Weill. Weill's clients included telecom companies and techs that were overpriced crap, which Grubman said very candidly in corporate emails while he hyped them to clients. For his trouble, Grubman was barred from the securities industry for life.[3] Another analyst with similar techniques was Henry Blodget, who was preened for his breed at ultrachic prep school Phillips Exeter and then at Yale. Banned from the securities industry for life, he became a publisher of — what else? — the *Business Insider*, which serves up news for business outsiders who want to think of themselves as within the gilded circles. His last legacy is a verb, "to blodget"; that is, to hype crap.[4] Playing on mass greed works for stocks as much as it does for massive lottery pots — the ones with $500 million jackpots — that induce otherwise sensible people to buy one or ten or hundreds of tickets for odds of winning that are infinitesimal. Folks just want to get in on the action.

The same mass mania is still a thriving part of peddling stocks. Corporate hype created by companies that fly analysts to show-and-tell extravaganzas, with resulting glowing reports of wealth to come, should be seen as suspect. When many analysts, usually on the sell side of the business, more or less simultaneously come up with breathless reports of fortunes to be made, the cautious investor should feel the hairs on the back of his or her neck rising. It is time for the serious investor who does not want to lose money to get out pencil and paper.

LOOKING BACK

There is no substitute for homework. Throwing years of savings at somebody else's concept with no homework is foolish. Homework begins with finding out how the company works and makes its money. And that is where accounting begins. Think of it as detective work, not bean counting. Every hour spent understanding a business is a defence against loss. It is the antidote to hype. And it is the very essence of understanding a public company as though it were your own business. Most of all, with a little work, it is interesting in the same way that a crossword puzzle is interesting. In each case, it is about filling in the spaces.

Accounting reports focus on the income statement: what the company shows for costs and sales; the balance sheet that summarized the assets, liabilities, and shareholder equity of the business; and the cash flow summary of money going in and out of the business. The cash flow statement is often overlooked by DIY investors but is the most useful tool to get a very good understanding of the health of the operations of a company. Each of these accounts is backward looking. Ideally, the past is prologue. We'll come to that later.

The cash flow statement is also a reality check, for if reported sales are rising and booked profits are going up while cash flow is shrinking, there needs to be some explanation. Companies can pre-sell goods and book what are really contingent orders not yet paid as sales, fattening revenue on the income statement, while showing shrinking cash flow. There are accounting rules against this, but it was done, famously, by Sunbeam Inc., which "sold" barbeques to hardware stores that had not ordered, much less paid for, them; booked the fictitious sales as revenue; deducted costs; and then asserted they had made profits. Point to watch: If receivables are rising faster than sales, something is wrong. The products are no good, shipping is a problem, the customers are broke, or consumers are returning goods very fast.[5]

> Every hour spent understanding a business is a defence against loss. It is the antidote to hype.

The value of a company is reflected in the income statement, balance sheet, and cash flow statement, but all that is past. There is more to a company than its financial history. If it were not so, then Polaroid Corp. would still be a thriving business and people would still be pecking away at Smith Corona typewriters. Neither company survived the technological shift to, respectively, digital imaging and word processing. Note that financial modelling cannot predict the future. Only clear thinking and imagination can do that.

KNOWLEDGE AND RISK

The question really comes down to what you know or can learn. Accounting statements need focus and concentration, but understanding business models takes forward thinking. The ratio of past to present can be found in some financial facts, such as whether a company is mature enough to pay and raise dividends. Yet for young firms in young industries, it is imagination that is key. Especially for early stage investments, one must deal with concept and how it is being executed. In our homespun example, it is whether the investor knows how their store works. It is so fundamental an idea that we have to ask why, in fact, people do throw money at companies whose operations and products they do not understand. If you own our paradigm small corner store, would you suddenly start selling auto parts or industrial solvents on the side? Profitable each may be, but the auto parts industry is one of many suppliers and huge inventory expenses — just look at any Canadian Tire parts rack — and industrial solvents have fire risk, zoning, and insurance costs that go along with being in the business of selling flammables. Car parts inventory costs would break the small store, and a spark from a tool being sharpened on a grinder could blow up everything. You would not do it. So why do it with your money without serious cost and risk analysis?

It is not so hard, given the abundance of research sources. A good deal of the homework the investor needs will be found in the company's accounts. For example, what are its assets? If they are real estate in good locations, there may be solid value. If the assets are intangibles like goodwill, or tough-to-value assets like trademarks, then facts become hopes and hopes can become dreams.[6] The risks a company faces can be learned in part from its liabilities. Are there a lot of loans coming due soon, and are there bonds that will have to be refinanced? Will the company retire bonds by issuing more shares, thus reducing earnings per share? Much of this is in published financial statements and each risk — refinancing and stock dilution — can be a warning to invest elsewhere.

The fundamental question is how profitable a company is. If it competes by cutting prices to the point that it makes no profits, then it will be destroying its own capital. Yet there are companies with falling sales but rising profits. Tobacco companies sell fewer cigarettes, yet their profits rise because of bans on costly advertising and the fundamental fact that nobody rushes to get into the cigarette business. The costs of entry and the risks from lawsuits are massive defences against new competitors.

You can tell how profitable a company is by looking at return on equity, ROE, which is net profit divided by equity. It shows how well a company's equity is used to generate a profit. You can also look at return on assets, which tends to be small when a company, such as a bank, has vast assets (its loans that generate interest) but makes only a small profit on loans.

The ROE varies by industry. For banks, 10 percent to 20 percent is normal; for pharmaceuticals, 20 percent to 40 percent reflects higher risks; for new entrants into high tech, it can be three digits, reflecting the high risks and brief lives of many new entrants.

For investors, there is more to life than chasing ROE or chasing dividends or returns on sales or any other single indicator. Financial analysts have come up with ever more intricate ways of looking at companies. We can cut through the growing complexity to make a few simple suggestions for getting returns and keeping capital safe:

> For investors, there is more to life than chasing ROE or dividends or any other single indicator.

1. Diversify. Have at least ten stocks in your portfolio and perhaps not more than two dozen. Above that, it is hard to follow the relevant news. Of course, if you use broad index funds, you get diversification at the cost of vast numbers of stocks you cannot name in some cases and certainly not track.
2. Make the foundation for your portfolio big companies that are widely followed in the financial press.
3. Be sure each firm has a long history of operation and — this is vital — of paying and raising dividends over the years.

Dividends and the ability to sustain and raise them reveal the health of a company. The higher the dividend expressed as yield or dividend per share, the better. But there can be companies that force up yield by paying out too much of their earnings or whose stock price is so low that the yield is attractive. Payouts over 80 percent of earnings raise warning signs, as do yields over 5 percent or 6 percent. In terms of our store, the operation should throw off cash for the owners after all employees and suppliers are paid and loans have been settled. However, if all earnings are paid out, what will be left for growth and expansion?

A revealing dividend statistic is the trend of payouts. If they are rising steadily, that is a good sign of profitability. If the dividend is small but growing, it will reward the buy-and-hold investor and tend to pump up the share price of the company. But beware. Some companies, especially resource businesses, cut their dividends when business languishes. For the income investor, a bouncing dividend is a warning sign to put money elsewhere.

John Maynard Keynes's analogy of likening investing in shares to a judge's task of picking a beauty contest winner on the basis of who the greatest number would think is prettiest, while unfortunately sexist, conveys the point that the stock market is a competition of companies seeking money. The most appealing companies can sell more shares and get more money per share sold than other firms seen as less attractive.

Over the long run and over a market cycle, the daily and weekly news, months-long trends, and even longer waves hardly matter.

There are other ways to handle the task of valuation. One way is to abandon hope and just buy a portfolio of shares in a market such as Toronto or New York. There are many packages of shares sold by companies that run exchange traded funds. When you buy an ETF, valuation problems are muted, and stock selection is done by some standard such as the top five hundred companies by capitalization in the S&P 500 or the Russell 2000's top two thousand U.S. companies ranked by capitalization. If you buy and hold and pay low fees, the market will be on your side. What is in daily newspapers will be rather unimportant, and reading business news will be at most a reason to take a headache pill on bad days and have a little champagne on good ones. Over the long run and over a market cycle, the daily and weekly news, months-long trends, and even longer waves hardly matter. The wobbly lines become straight vectors. Sleep is easy if you take this view.

In the end, it is short- to medium-term risk that we have to evaluate. Risk is mirrored in liquidity. The more easily an asset trades, that is, the more frequently and with smaller gaps between bid and ask, the more market price will reflect investors' views. But liquidity itself rises with investor enthusiasm and tends to fall when investors have neither interest in an asset nor, perhaps, money to spend.

In periods of great enthusiasm, as there was in the dot-com mania of the late 1990s, investors could and did abandon good sense. What was called the "burn rate" captivated small investors who were persuaded by articles in the press and statements by portfolio managers that the faster a new company ate up its capital, the better the prospects of the business. This was nonsense, and, as you might imagine, any small store owner who decided to burn their store — forget the criminal penalties and insurance claim rejection — or eat up their inventory or perhaps just give their capital away would be bust. Not surprisingly, high burn rates led to just that. Yet in the anonymity of the stock market, high burn rates were welcomed, not least because companies burning their capital would have to return to the trough to get more money to burn. The moral: Beware investment bankers and their handmaiden sell-side analysts who turn the implausible into virtue. Rely on your own good sense. Destruction of capital is bad. Period.

Last of all, we should mention the way some investors and even portfolio managers pick stocks and bonds — so-called technical analysis. Done with points on graph paper that represent daily or other period prices, the dots are connected and patterns observed. Those who do this work call themselves "technicians," and some add insight to investing. However, the patterns they find, such as what they call head and shoulders formations, only appear with prices observed daily or weekly. They are submerged in long moving averages and are hard to find with very short period observations; for example, minute-by-minute tracks in the digital dust. If the graphing medium is logarithmic, the patterns are skewed. You could say that visualization cannot be bad, but when the image depends on observation periods and the way lines are separated on graph paper, the question arises: Why should any asset's proper price be revealed by day or by any other period? Nevertheless, the faithful follow this school of finding truth in lines. At best, it is financial wizardry. It can show investor enthusiasm. At worst, it is a kind of financial necromancy not so different from Shakespeare's witches seeking truth from a boiling kettle of unfortunate newts, frogs, and lizards.

Yet one can defend technical analysis as top-down in contrast to the bottom-up methods of examining accounts and other components of so-called fundamental analysis. Popularity does support stock and other asset prices, and lack of popularity can crush prices. But popularity alone does not rule, and the recent past says little about the distant future. One may object that fundamental analysis also does not capture the future, but it can. For regulated utilities with long lives, there is some sense of distant continuity. It is the asset base and perhaps the intelligence of management that will keep BCE Inc. generating dividends for decades to come. Crowd opinion is just cheering (or not) from the bleachers.

Dot-coms no longer can burn cash with abandon now that the stock market has refused to provide fresh fuel. But in the long run, these ventures may be better served by the new focus on such Old Economy nostrums as profitability.

In juggling methods of finding the true value of a share of stock, which is the bottom-up style most often taught in business schools, and the market polling technique of technical analysis, which seeks to find a consensus among investors by what amounts to polling, there are numerous tests for momentum; that is, rate of gain or loss of value in a given time period, assessment of the inner business of banks to find the worth of their loans. This is a price-to-book (value) process, and more, the investor can be overwhelmed by numbers.

WHAT MATTERS, WHAT DOESN'T

The question the befuddled investor has to ask is which of many variables matter a lot and which either matter little or are reflected in the movement of other variables. The distinguished corporate value researcher and teacher Aswath Damodaran, professor of finance at New York University's Stern School of Business, suggests that the investor focus not on the great swath of trends, but on what is to be explained. If it is total returns or returns excess of some marker such as the average of companies in a certain industry, the gap needs to be explained.[7]

The next important decision is to determine what period or interval will be chosen. It could be monthly, quarterly, annually, or over periods of years. The returns can be smoothed into multi-period averages. Given that quarterly numbers can be quite jumpy, the investor may choose to average them or to use annual numbers.

It is helpful to do all this with pencil and graph paper. You get a feel for the numbers that a computer spreadsheet won't provide. The computer can generate studies and relationships with the push of a button, but if the idea is to seek simplicity, fancy math is not going to help.

Finally, there is the problem of verifying a theory. If you find that automobile sales predict sales of tires, for example, you have a problem of what statisticians call — forgive this, but it is true — autocorrelation. Tire sales can as well predict car sales, for each car comes with four or five tires and some trucks with more tires. The fact that tire sales correlate with car sales has no predictive value. Indeed, if replacement tires are counted, it is possible that higher tire sales predict lower new car sales. It is not numbers that rule; it is common sense.

> Number crunching can be an investor's enemy if it is not used with common sense.

Number crunching can be an investor's enemy if it is not used with common sense. In market prediction, there are two great scenarios: first, that stocks will go up, and second, that they will fall. In this seemingly idiotic classification is a kernel of complexity, for when you collect high-risk stocks, such as junior oil companies that live or die on their drilling successes or lack of them, the returns, risks included, seem to be higher than those of integrated oil companies that drill, refine, and sell petroleum products. Higher-than-average risk correlates with lower-than-average survival. Lower-than-average risk correlates with higher-than-average survival. That is as it should be.

SURVIVOR BIAS

Companies that fold up or go bankrupt drop out of the ongoing data, leaving just the survivors, which, of course, did not have the bad luck or foolish management, drilling failures, or whatever that caused failure. The same problem of survivor bias, discussed in depth in Chapter 1, arises with deep value stocks; that is, those with low price-to-earnings ratios. Many have low ratios not because investors are wrong, but because they are right and take their money out. The failure rate among deep value stocks is higher than that of the market as a whole. You could say this just shows that the dead don't talk.

Over the decades since it was established in 1896, the Dow Jones Industrial Average has had many changes in the thirty stocks it tracks. None of the twelve industrials in the index in 1896 is still isted in the Dow Jones Inustrial Average. The last survivor, General Electric Company, was dropped from the list of the venerables on June 19, 2018, and replaced with the Walgreens Boots Alliance drug store chain. All the other originals died or were swapped for newer or more successful companies. To say that the Dow has risen from a level of 140 in 1928 to 25,000 as I write this, 180 times its original value, is to miss the point. The index managers have successfully picked winners and thrown out losers. Today's value is little more than survivor bias.

> The problem of survivor bias raises the question of which screens for enduring value actually work.

What is true for the DJIA is also true for the S&P 500, which is managed by bringing in winners and kicking out losers. And by the essence of identity, it is true for any list of European banks, which is a list of survivors and a *shhh* list of failures, Russian energy firms allowed to exist by the government, and fashion goods companies that have not failed.

The problem of survivor bias raises the question of which screens for enduring value actually work. Companies drop in and out of indices; mutual funds that have one or another theory live and thrive or just get merged into others, with the result that the losers' operating theories are no longer tested.

ENDURING VALUE

Enduring value has to be the quest, especially for buy-and-hold investors. The American classical scholar and, later, investor Benjamin Graham pondered the problem of finding enduring value. During the Great Depression of 1929 to 1938, he wrote, with David Dodd, *Security Analysis*, the book that created the discipline of analyzing stocks for intrinsic value.[8]

Graham identified many signals of good value. We can't use them today in their original form, for ratios and numbers have changed in the last eight decades, but we can observe the ideas. For Graham, a promising stock had, among other things, a ratio of price to earnings less than six for the last five years. The stock price could not be more than two-thirds of tangible book value (book value less intangibles such as goodwill), price could not be less than two-thirds of net current asset value (liquid current assets including cash minus current liabilities), and historical growth in earnings per share had to be 7 percent or more for each year of the last ten years. These ratios would be hard to satisfy today, but the concept is really just accounting applied to find intrinsic value. Yet one of Graham's students has used his teacher's methods to generate the greatest investment fortune in America and surely one of the greatest in the world. That's Warren Buffett.

Buffett has been studied and lionized for decades, yet his core concepts fit perfectly with our idea that the investor should do their own homework and understand their portfolio as thoroughly as they would a small business. For Buffett, a business he might buy would have to be understandable and basically simple. It should have a consistent operating history, favourable long-term prospects, and trustworthy management. In the end, Buffett wants a business and his portfolio to be steady even when his opponent, Mr. Market, is moody and variously frivolous or self-destructive.

GROWTH MODELS

Growth investing is, in some senses, the antithesis of value investing. Rather than try to find stocks with low ratios of price to earnings or price to book, which is essentially a quest for prices lower than they perhaps should be, growth investors worry relatively little about the "p" and concentrate instead on the "e." Small cap stocks tend to be growth stocks. The reason is both in their perceived potential and the simple arithmetic proposition that it is easier for a company with $10 million in earnings to add another million than for a company with $10 billion in earnings to add another billion.

Most stocks on major exchanges were once small cap growth companies. Today, there are many small caps for the asking, many emerging as initial public offerings (IPOs for short) with sales commissions paid by the underwriters and by the company itself but ultimately by the investors whose money is eroded by investment bankers by 5 percent to 7 percent or up to 20 percent or more for little stocks that wind up on so-called pink sheets for low volume, hide-and-seek companies.

IPO trolling is often a swamp in which the innocent get eaten by the connected. The idea is that one can buy into the IPO as a ground-floor investment, with the brokerage fee paid by the company launching the shares. The fee is indeed paid, but that is where the bargain ends.

In the dot-com era from 1998 to 2000, it was common for companies' IPOs to be so underpriced and investor interest so keen that new shares would hit the market — usually by sales to favoured or large clients and mutual funds — and then rise by 30 percent or 50 percent or more in an hour. Companies with shares so underpriced were deprived of capital, and late investors who got shares the first owners were dumping then took losses. IPOs were no place for innocents; the stories of huge profits were true — but true mainly for insiders. Today, IPOs have been tamed, and ridiculous pricing is less common. But the rule that they help the connected and hurt the innocent remains true.

> The knack required of the growth investor is the ability to spot companies with prospects better than those the market has ascribed to them.

Whatever the source of stock, whether IPO or seasoned shares, the knack required of the growth investor is the ability to spot companies with prospects better than those the market has ascribed to them. This is not so easy as it may seem. The wizards of corporate finance who put IPOs together can craft business models for firms that are nothing more than dreams. Sales can be specified to grow at 50 percent a year or 25 percent or 60 percent — whatever a bit of pencil work can devise, then costs and profits as a fraction of those sales, then predicted taxes, returns for investors, and more. Much of this is numerical fiction. Many IPOs that launch fail to raise money sought, even more drown their investors in subsequent losses by the companies, and still more reward investment industry players like mutual funds with good connections and professional investors who buy at the opening, hold an hour or two, and reap profits. Small investors and outsiders have little chance of getting into the IPOs at early prices.

It is true that Apple and Microsoft were once IPOs, but so were Seco Holding Ltd — ADR (symbol: SECO), a Chinese company that lost 23 percent of its value on its first day on the NASDAQ. Priced at US$12 at launch in 2017, it had a minus 9.9 percent return for the year ended December 31, 2017. The problem for the would-be investor in the IPO is to discern how it will trade. With no history, perhaps no analysts following it, and no track record on public markets, it is a crap shoot. Actually, the odds in craps are better.

On a risk and return basis, IPOs are chancier than seasoned stocks with long histories of life in up and down markets and known histories of issuing and increasing dividends, living with legislation, and paying taxes. The early and lucky entrant into a company via an IPO may do very well. Or lose his or her shirt. With the exception of freshly created exchange traded funds that are stocked in most cases with seasoned shares, IPOs are traps for the innocent who are tempted by what seem to be fresh opportunities backed by clever marketing and the offer of a purchase with no sales fee. There is novelty in getting in on the ground floor, but the reality is that after the favoured early buyers sell, shares can and often do tumble in price.

RISK MANAGEMENT

Both value investing and growth investing require some detective work. In either case, one can scan databases to find companies with very low p/e's or high dividend yields over, say, 6 percent. If the "p" is low, then one has to find out why. If the "e" is growing, likewise, one needs to know why.

Risk is in the eye of the beholder, but in balancing value investing in stocks with low p/e's, on the theory they are unduly cheap, and growth investing in those with high p/e's, on the theory that their e's are not appreciated by other investors, cheap is safer than racing. After all, if a company is solvent and you can buy it for a p/e of 12, it may fall 50 percent to a p/e of 6. But a growth stock with a p/e of 50 can lose 80 percent of its value in a fortnight, even in one night, and drop to a p/e of 10. It is said that while value investors need patience, growth investors need guts. And that is just about right.

In choosing which strategy to follow, one can observe that cheap is better for performance and certainly better for safety. There is a middle ground, growth at a reasonable price, commonly called GARP. Often expressed as the PEG ratio, it compares the p/e to the growth rate. So, dividing p/e by growth rate, a p/e of 10 and a growth rate of 30 percent, for example, would have a PEG ratio of 0.33. Anything less than 1 is good, and anything over 1 is not good in this conception. A stock with a p/e of 50 and growth of 10 percent a year would have a PEG ratio of 5 — a sign of an over-priced stock. The use of low PEG ratios has been found by academic researchers to produce higher returns than would be obtained with high PEG ratios. This would be the end of the story were it not for the problem that the "e" component is in both the numerator and the divisor. So the equation in rough terms turns out to be a quest for cheap stocks. That is value investing and, of course, it tends to work. Use PEGs as you like, but do not rely on them as final tests of value. They are filters, perhaps. They are echoes, for sure.

It is said that while value investors need patience, growth investors need guts. And that is just about right.

NON-FINANCIAL INDICATORS

The accounting work we have discussed is not so different from what any small business owner may do with a business when it comes to buying out a competitor. The problem is to determine what the business to be acquired is worth.

Bean counting has its place, of course. But there is another way akin to what you might do if asked to set a price on a business: find out what the management is doing. It's a cinch with public companies.

Ownership and Trading by Management and Directors

For every public company, directors' interests — the shares they hold — will be listed in the annual documentation sent to shareholders. Moreover, when directors and senior managers buy or sell shares, it's reported and accessible via investment databases like SEDAR (sedar.com) and its American cousin, EDGAR (sec.gov/edgar). If you follow the financial press, major moves in and out of company shares held by insiders will be available. Searching a database before buying is fast and only reasonable. Some share sales will be for "estate planning," which may be true or may be a cop out for getting the hell out before the ceiling falls in.

This question as to what the directors and top managers are doing probes the key question for long-term investors: Is this a business you would like to own a very long time? It is said to be the question at the core of the valuation process of Warren Buffett. His technique of valuation, learned in classes taught by Benjamin Graham, as previously noted, is not exotic, not reliant on fancy math or exacting statistical tests. It's just common sense that can bridge bad quarters and new product misses like the Coca-Cola Company's launch of what was called New Coke in the 1980s and, more recently, its launch of a formulation called Coke Life, with a new sweetener. The stuff, marketed in the U.K., comes in a green can. Sales are a fizzle, but Coke is not going to fail, and its shares are priced at time of writing with a multiple of 23 times trailing profits, a little higher than Pepsico's 21 multiple over trailing earnings. Coke has a 3.3 percent yield, Pepsico a 3.2 percent yield. A few cans of weird glop sold in one market won't kill this great corporation.

Share Buybacks

Stockholders love share buybacks because they can sell their stock, often without commission, and get a good price while holding remaining shares that, because there are fewer of them, wind up with more earnings per share than before, when there were more shares. Higher EPS drives up the value of underlying stock. Executive compensation plans based on share price or EPS reward the managers with higher pay or bonuses. Everybody is happy.

And yet, if the money for the buyout comes from earnings that might better have been used in the business, the buyback may be not so rosy after all. If the company sells bonds to get cash to buy shares, then the balance sheet is impaired and the company will in some measures be worth less.

Very low interest rates stimulated buybacks in 2014 and 2015. The directors approving the deals figured that if they could borrow at historically low rates of 2 percent or less, as some global names did, shifting to debt financing and away from equity financing was a good idea. Moreover, because bond and other debt interest comes off income statements before the bottom line, they are tax-advantaged. Dividends are paid out of earnings and are not directly deductible from earnings. Deductibility can be made to work with very complex ownership structures, but those structures, if not understood, are actually a reason to invest elsewhere.

Trade Journals

If you want the inside track on the hair removal industry, you should read *International Hair Route Magazine*, with offices in Canada and the United States. There are specialist magazines that track the Russian cement business, such as *Cement and Its Applications* (Russian language only, sorry); *Servo Magazine*, with a column on rubber bands and bailing wire; and *Lapidary Journal Jewelry Artist*, for insights into such things as diamond use.

Forensic Methods

There have been famous undoings of big companies achieved by detective work. Some of this is in the realm of forensic accounting, the results of which come to light when a company turns out to be variously optimistic in its reports or downright fraudulent. One can compare production figures with sales and shipments in financial statements to find vast amounts of goods made but not sold in spite of quarterly and annual reports that tout sales bonanzas.[9] Sunbeam Corp., a maker of barbeques, among other things, was taken over by a corporate accounting artiste named Al Dunlap. Called "Chainsaw" for his style of firing workers to cut costs and then fictionalizing sales, he recorded as sold goods neither shipped nor received by customers. This method boosted accounting profits but was deeply deceptive. Forensic accountants and sleuths could and did uncover his methods. A method for scouting frauds can be found in *The Sleuth Investor* by Avner Mandelman.[10]

BONDS AND THEIR WORTH

We need to talk about bond valuation as well. We'll go into this more in the bond chapter, but bonds, which are promises to pay made by governments or corporations and, in a few cases, international institutions, tend to return less than stocks. They are more strictly built on accounts and less on expectations because they carry less risk. Bondholders are in line ahead of common and preferred stockholders in bankruptcy and when corporate cash is payed out. Moreover, bondholders have a contractual promise to be paid specific sums or according to specific formulas. Stockholders just have the collective will of the directors, who may and sometimes do change their minds and reduce or eliminate dividends.

Bond valuation is a numerical process similar to that of stocks when it comes to figuring out what a company is worth, but it is more focused on the balance sheet and on the few lines of the annual report that show how much money is available for payment of bonds. The valuation exercise is not needed for bonds of national governments, for they can print money if they must to pay bond coupons and to repay bond principal. For corporate bonds, what works for stockholders also works for bond holders, and there are credit rating agency reports for domestic and foreign governments and corporations online.

One of the shortest analytical processes is to compare bond descriptions and analysts' comments for various categories of bonds. For U.S. Treasury bonds, Government of Canada bonds, and the obligations of the Bank of England, Germany's Bundesbank, and the Bank of Japan, to name a few, there is nothing that has to be said. The bonds will be paid on time. That's it. For Canadian provincial bonds, there is not a lot to say, though analysts prattle on. If any province were in trouble, the other provinces and the federal government would go to bat for the weakling. If they did not, the national market would be ruined. No province has defaulted since the Great Depression.

Get into corporations and there are more words. There are not so many in most bond reports for giants like telco BCE Inc., and can pay bond interest out of its vast revenues. There are more words for big railroads dependent on traffic, and long explanations for the finances of bond-issuing car makers and grocery chains, big oil companies, and banks with complex businesses. Get into junk bonds and the stories get longer. In convertible bonds, the stories can become short books. In bond analysis, the less said, the better.

For high-quality bonds of governments and corporations, inflation matters greatly in bond analysis. If it rises, new bonds will come out with higher rates of interest and the prices of old bonds will fall until the ratio of interest divided by price matches that of new, higher interest bonds. If a company issuing bonds has a very bad year, the risk of default the market perceives will cause its bonds' prices to fall. However, good-quality bonds held to maturity for ten years or less are not very risky, and, within limits, they can go into a portfolio.

In bond analysis, the less said in bond descriptions and analysts' comments, the better.

The value of bonds in a portfolio is that they tend to be inversely related to stock prices, so when stocks swoon, bonds usually rise. Yet over the long run, say periods of five or more years, bond returns are less than stock returns. Indeed, for the period from 1802 to 2012, stocks beat bonds 68 percent of the time for five-year holding periods, 72 percent of the time for ten-year holding periods, 84 percent of the time for twenty-year holding periods, and 99 percent of the time for thirty-year holding periods. In that 210-year period, stocks had an average annual real gain of 6.6 percent, while bonds only gained 3.6 percent and gold just 0.7 percent, and cash lost 1.4 percent per year.[11] The case for bonds appears weak, but a two-century cycle is too long in reality. A lifespan of 50 years as an adult investor is long enough. In that period, there will be perhaps eight to ten stock cycles and half that number of bond cycles. Weaving the two asset classes together provides not only some portfolio stability but also the psychological comfort that, if stocks are falling, bonds will rise and provide a measure of compensation. That could be done with stock options, but they are complex, take active monitoring, and complicate portfolio management. Bonds, at least, are simple keepers.

Bonds are rated by agencies including Fitch, S&P, Moody's, and DBRS with letters and numbers that, in general, go from A to C and then to D. A+ is tops, C- is near default, and D (for distressed) is in default.

The simplest idea of a bond is payment of interest yearly or semi-annually and repayment of principal at maturity. Other bonds are linked to inflation rates, with payouts rising as inflation increases or falling when inflation drops. Bonds that pay nothing until their maturity or due date are riskier than bonds that pay progressively. Famously used by Canadian construction magnate Robert Campeau in his ill-fated and some say doomed takeover of Federated and Allied department stores in the late 1980s, the bonds paid no interest until maturity and ultimately were worthless.[12]

The end of the story is this: high-yield bonds or junk bonds are not necessarily bad. They may be risky or just not rated, for the rating agencies charge a great deal for their work. The investor must understand the issuer's balance sheet and ability to pay interest. They are intrinsically sounder than stock, for the interest has to be paid someday. Even so, the mortality rates for junk are astronomical. Only about half ever make it to maturity without default, in contrast to high investment grade bonds, including government bonds issued by the U.S. Treasury, the Government of Canada, and other sovereigns and sub-sovereign units like provinces, which almost never default.

Bonds are different from stocks in that the investor is merely a money lender. Government bonds are largely riskless on default. Non-government bonds need analysis and, because of capital requirements for the banks that used to make markets in bonds, they are hard to trade. Our advice: By all means buy bonds if you need them to stabilize a portfolio, for yield, or for diversification. But use a bond mutual fund with a low fee or a bond exchange traded fund. It's a professional's game in which non-professionals have a very hard time beating traders or institutional investors.

WHAT YOU KNOW AND WHAT YOU DON'T

Good students of Nicholas Nassim Taleb's *Black Swan* quote his turkey maxim that life is good for the birds.[13] People bring food to eat, and there is water and some veterinary care. The turkey management department assures the member turkeys that life is stable. Then, as Thanksgiving approaches, the outlook changes. Experience is a good teacher, but it is of limited value in a universe of instability.

So, too, in investing. Forward vision is everything. It failed Kodak, which did not see how deeply digital imaging would cut into its business of film photography. The same problem exists for almost every other business, for change is inevitable. So, as you would for your small store, buy what you know, but allow for expansion into what you do not know. Expand only to the point that previous profits pay for the greater cost of more risk. Rely on the familiar, experiment with the unfamiliar to the point that it becomes familiar, then add to risk capital. What is known is not all that can be known.

> Rely on the familiar, experiment with the unfamiliar to the point that it becomes familiar, then add to risk capital.

Beware the black holes of knowledge. Accounting and statistics only cope with the past. The future is the problem. To rush to get in on the latest thing, which is the marijuana grow-op craze now that it has been or is being legalized in many jurisdictions, is to forget what has to be the investor's base motto: Just don't do anything stupid. Conservative investing in stocks with a history, modest or reasonable prices in terms of past and expected earnings, dependable dividends, and conservatively estimated growth prospects are not the way to quick riches. But they are far less likely to cause losses than investing in stocks with no dividends, no history, long stories, heavy promotion, and little to show for it. Concepts are splendid, but you cannot take them to the bank.

CHAPTER 4

Bonds: Evaluating the Risks of Return of Your Capital

Long ago, before the wizards of Wall Street and Bay Street invented synthetic bonds and turned pyramids of debt into $10 million annual bonuses, fixed income meant bonds. You put down as little as $25 for a savings bond or $1,000 for a corporate bond, clipped the coupons, got your interest, and, at the bond's maturity, took the bond back to the bank or investment dealer to redeem the face value. With government bonds and highest grade corporate bonds, the odds of payment at maturity and at coupon dates along the way were about 100 percent.

It may not have been much, but it was foolproof. If you lost your bond, the Bank of Canada or the U.S. Treasury would replace it. Bonds were life preservers when riskier assets such as stocks sank out of sight. In that sense, they were, and in pure form remain, insurance policies of a kind, but they are more, for, bought for the right reasons and at the right times, they can generate tidy profits while preserving their essential character — the promise to pay interest and to repay their principal.

Bonds traditionally pay less than stocks, although, structurally, genuine investment grade bonds — as opposed to synthetic bonds made of other bonds or debts or junk bonds of companies analysts think might default before maturity — are almost always secure. The question of whether the security intrinsic in a quality bond is worth the reduced return as compared to a stock has been as finely examined as the parable of figuring out how many angels can fit on the head of a pin. For the practical investor, the question remains: Is it worth it to have bonds? And if so, how much and which ones?

How much of a bond position to hold is subject to much debate. A conventional formula suggests that one deduct one's age from one hundred to set the stock allocation of a portfolio. At fifty, you can be 50 percent in stocks, 50 percent in bonds. At seventy, stocks will be 30 percent of the portfolio, bonds 70 percent. This is only a rule of thumb. It is based on government bonds that have almost no chance of default, and it need not be followed blindly. If you hold investment-grade corporate bonds, which have some linkage to how stocks fare, then you can raise the bond allocation and drop the stock portion, for there is stock-ness in the bonds. If you have sub-investment grade corporate bonds, a.k.a. junk, then the low-grade bonds should be treated as stock, for they rise and fall with stocks along with variations of government bonds. The junkier the bond, the more its price wobbles like the stock of the issuing company.

> For the practical investor, the question remains: Is it worth it to have bonds? And if so, how much and which ones?

WHAT'S A BOND?

A bond, technically speaking, is a loan usually made by many people to one company or government. The loan is collectible in the form of a set number of interest payments and repayment of the principal at a specific date. The bond may be callable before maturity. This means that the issuer can cut short the life of the bond and terminate interest payments. Call features usually mean that the bond with this twist will pay a little more than one without it. Calls are common on corporate bonds, for they can limit costs for the issuer if interest rates decline and the issuer would like to refinance at a lower cost.

A few bonds, called perpetuals, have no final payment date. Bonds of this kind called "consols" were used to finance Britain's costs in the Napoleonic wars. These days, perpetual bonds are very rare, though there are many perpetual preferred shares. Other bonds, called amortizers, pay their principal back at regular intervals so that at maturity there is very little of the bond's face value outstanding. Whatever the type of bond, and with few exceptions, it is a solemn promise to make periodic payments and to return principal at a fixed date or, in the case of a perpetual, some unspecified day in future. Those promises are enforceable by holders who can take the issuer to court and seize factories or office buildings, bank accounts, or anything else if they are not paid. That promise works with corporate bonds, though with bonds of governments, especially national governments with armies, it can be hard to seize assets. However, even with defaulting dictatorships, it has been done when a president's plane is within the grasp of the bondholders' lawyers. We're making this little foray into bondholders' rights to show the difference with stocks, for holders of shares of any company have no rights other than to elect directors. It is a world of difference.

That difference explains why bonds usually pay less than stocks. But that does not mean that bonds are not profitable. Indeed, long before there was the idea of ownership of businesses via issues of shares of stock — that's little more than 400 years old — there were bonds and methods for enforcement of payment. We can trace the parts of bonds, such as enforcement of payment, back to Hammurabi in 1800 B.C. In a more recent time — if we can call something in the early seventeenth century recent — a Dutch woman, one Elsken Jorisdochter, bought 1,200 florins worth of perpetual bonds paying about 6 1/4 percent per year. They were issued by the Lekdyk Bovendams Company, a public utility business chartered in 1323, which was essentially a state corporation able to raise money by taxation. The bonds' payments could not be taxed — thus, they were similar to certain U.S. municipal bonds in their state of issue. It was what we would call a Crown corporation. The bonds were bought and sold until the last recorded trade in 1957.

VALUING A BOND

A bond is a solemn promise to pay. Issuers like to borrow through bonds because once the loan to the company is complete — that is, once the bond is sold and the investment banks have taken their piece, often 3 to 6 percent of the total borrowed — repayment is up to the issuing company. There are no pesky bankers to ask about the company maintaining this or that ratio of costs to sales, reserves for bad debts, et cetera. Holders can sell if they don't like how the borrower is handling its affairs. The covenants that come with the bond lay out the rules, but once sold, the bond is usually just a cost to the issuer with interest deductible from income.

There are two components to bond value. For government bonds, especially sovereigns like U.S. Treasuries or Government of Canada bonds, ability to pay is not an issue. There are no credit questions. The only issue is sensitivity to interest rate changes. This is called duration, really a misnomer, though you can think of it as how long it takes to get your money back.

Interest rate sensitivity calculations are usually a piece of fancy calculus called Macaulay duration, after the professor who worked it out. For a strip bond, as it is called in Canada, or a zero, as it is called in the U.S., duration equals term. That is, if the strip is due in thirty years, duration is thirty, and the way it works is that a 1 percent rise in interest rates will cut 30 percent off the bond's value — the strip's price in this case. Alternatively, a 1 percent fall in interest rates will make the bond rise 30 percent in price. This assumes no trading costs or commissions. For shorter terms, the duration calculation will express the time weighted returns relative to interest rates. There is an easy to use duration calculator online at investopedia.com/calculator/bonddurcdate.aspx.

Interest on corporate bonds is often expressed as yield to maturity and yield to worst, which means the call if, like many corporate bonds, the issuer can demand outstanding bonds be returned, usually with a little bonus.

The other component of bond value is the chance of default. For AAA bonds, which are as rare as that old cliché, hen's teeth, default is considered remote. That is about right for all bonds with A ratings. Go to the Bs and the chance of default rises. A diligent investor in any fixed income security, whether a bond or a preferred stock or even a short-term promissory debt (called a "note" if it is due in a year or less), should read the covenants. They are available online at the Canadian SEDAR website or at the U.S. EDGAR site. It is boring but essential reading. If a bond is rated BBB or below, you must read the covenants. They spell out the terms of the loan and investor rights. Covenants are sleep inducing. Hundreds of pages of disclosures and conditions and what ifs.

But there is a shortcut to all this.

If a bond is issued by a government that can print money, there is no story, and the covenants, though they exist, are not worth reading. The federal governments of Canada and the U.S. and the

> A diligent investor in any fixed income security should read the covenants.

Bank of England are not going to default. Their bonds have top investment grade ratings, AAA or close to it for some U.S. agency bonds and some parts of Canada's public debt. There may be a few quibbles, but worry not — they are solid credits. Subnational governments such as provinces could default, but they have the power to tax. Some American states and territories — think of Puerto Rico — are insolvent. Indeed, Puerto Rico defaulted on July 1, 2016. Before Hurricane Maria in September 2017, the island was already over $70 billion in debt — about $20,000 per island resident. The disorganized relief efforts of the Trump administration are unlikely to reduce this debt. Holders of Puerto Rico government bonds will have to wait many years to be made whole and may, in fact, have to settle for less than full payment of their bonds. It is not just Puerto Rico. Bonds issued by the State of Illinois were downgraded to near junk levels by Moody's Investor Services and S&P Global Ratings in mid-2017. Illinois's ten-year bonds yielded 4.4 percent, 2.5 percentage points more than those on top-rated debt at the end of May 2017. That spread — a measure of the perceived risk — is more than any of the other nineteen states tracked by Bloomberg. The lesson here is that you *must* research any outfit to which you consider lending money. Even if the payoff is a lot more than a more financially solid entity pays, it is not a gift. Higher yields in bonds always reflect higher risk. To avoid the casino effect, which is losing your bet, do your research.

For any corporation, default is possible. So here is our rule: The shorter the story, the more solid the bond. If you are down in C bonds, the story has to be read closely. You are buying junk debt and you need to know the rules. C bonds have a better than 50/50 chance of default before maturity at ten or more years. Thus, the rule: The longer the story, the crummier the bond. If a bond is secured by air rights, think twice before investing. Seizing air is tough. Claiming the right to build on top of another building is possible. But this is literally airy fairy investing. If you want a solid asset, air and a long story are not what you are seeking.

For every wiggle of rating for every bond there is a price adjustment, and even defaulted bonds, called "distressed" in the bond biz, can and do trade for pennies on the dollar on the chance that holders, who often employ armies of lawyers to collect their money, will be able to squeeze cash from what appear to be dry wells. In fact, by seizing assets and even by use of political pressure, ransacked companies and bankrupt governments can be made to pay through asset sales or seizures. The theory is that if you can buy a distressed bond for pennies on the dollar, then, with sufficient legal muscle, you can profit handsomely. Novice investors need not go here, it should be said.

One of the most egregious cases of a bond default is still in the process of settlement after twenty years of litigation, attempts to seize the foreign debtor's assets, monstrous legal fees amounting to hundreds of millions of dollars, and, no doubt, the deaths of many of the investors who tossed what was reported to be their life savings into the bonds. It is the long-running but winding-down case of the Argentine bond default, the biggest ever so far. It was the eighth time the country had defaulted on its bonds since it established its independence in 1816.

The case began in 1998 when Argentina went into recession. Short of tax revenues, the nation defaulted on a whopping US$93 billion of bonds held mostly by foreigners. The move was shortsighted, for foreign investment rushed for the exits and new money stayed out of Argentina. Not worrying about debts was the legacy of Juan Peron, the populist strongman who ruled the country from 1946 to 1955 and then from 1973 to 1974. He borrowed heavily from foreign investors, inflated the currency, and, for all that, was overshadowed by his wife, Eva, considered by some Argentinians to be the reincarnation of the Virgin Mary. The truth: Eva, an "entertainer" before she married Juan, was not exactly a saint; Peron, an admirer of Mussolini and host to many top German war criminals, was no fair-minded democrat; and his government was a kleptocracy held together by what amounted to bank robbery. The concepts of Peronism have pervaded successor governments. Argentina remains a developing country risk in the bond market, and Peron's machismo fronting for populism is now the style of the ruinous government of Venezuela, once the richest country by per capita income in South America and now the poorest.

The default hurt not only professional investors, but also the relatives of many Argentinians who had taken up residence overseas. Others were former Argentinians who had bought their mother country's debt out of a feeling of loyalty. The government of Argentina then stopped supporting the national currency, the peso, and it fell from one to one with the U.S. dollar to 25 U.S. cents. That jacked up inflation to 40 percent, and the nation's gross domestic product fell by 10 percent in 2002.

Creditors went hunting for overseas Argentine assets. They tried to seize the airplane of the president of Argentina and one Argentine warship (this failed because of sovereign immunity). Argentina countered and offered investment funds and individual holders payments if they would accept settlement at what was just about a dime on the dollar. Many investment funds took debt swaps, accepting long-term Argentine bonds at low rates — the best deals they could get. Holdouts went to court in the U.S. Speculators moved in, buying Argentine defaulted bonds for pennies on the dollar. One hedge fund manager was reported to have made 3,000 percent on the deeply discounted bonds. In the end, by 2016, almost all of the debt, which, with interest, had reached a value of US$100 billion, was paid. The cost of lawsuits in the U.S. and in European litigation is not known but was surely in the billions. The moral of the story is that recovering money from a defaulted bond issued in any fancy deal involving a foreign nation with an army and a navy will be tough going.

Is there a warning flag? When the yield on any commercial or international bond, which is the expected interest divided by current or recent market price, goes to two or three times or more the yield on U.S. Treasury debt of the same term, don't buy. For small countries with no clear ways to earn U.S. dollars or other global currencies the bonds may be issued in, high interest rates are a sign the bond price has fallen. In the world financial crisis following the 2008 mortgage meltdown, Greek sovereign bond yields went as high as 40 percent if any seller could get a bid. Anytime the yield on a corporate bond or a foreign government bond gets to a few hundred basis points (there are 100 basis points in one percentage point) over the yield on ten-year Government of Canada or U.S. Treasury bonds, watch out. At 500 basis points over senior bonds' yields, the suspect bond is priced for danger. At 800 basis points or more, the market is sure the bond will never make it to maturity and probably won't pay interest much longer.

> If a bond's promised return is many times that of a U.S. or Canadian investment-grade bond, save yourself tears — stay away.

Argentina was a worst case, for its external debt rose to 447 times its exports in 1982. It could not pay its national debt. The default was inevitable. Other debtor countries that defaulted were Morocco, with external debt 305 times exports, and Guyana, with its debts 338 times exports. Default by struggling governments is common, especially if they have to earn foreign exchange like U.S. dollars to pay the bonds.[1] Use a bond's market price as a measure of its risk. When the coupon interest rate divided by market price boosts coupon yield to multiples of the yield on top-ranked global bonds, invest elsewhere if you want to sleep well at night.

READING BOND TEA LEAVES

There is a moral to this tale of risky bonds: the longer the story that a bond has, the riskier it is. Government of Canada bonds and U.S. Treasury bonds have no story. Their value is mostly dependent on interest rates now, what investors think rates may be in future, and inflation expectations. They will pay on time, every coupon and every face value certificate — though bonds and coupons are no longer issued in paper. When bonds get into junk territory or come with a bonus piece of stock attached — these are convertible bonds — the stories are long and the math to figure out what they are worth is demanding.

The best way to figure the value of a bond in the broadest sense is what government or top-notch corporate debt can do for you over long periods of time. Government bonds, which rule the roost of debt, are bulletproof when issued by the best of nations — that's best in a financial sense, not any other. Stocks, on the other hand, are not bulletproof and they are very seldom issued by governments, save for the rare occasions when Crown corporations go public — the CNR is an example — or when governments back private ventures — as is the case of Ontario's Highway 407, a public/private venture.

Now consider what stocks have done when investors are swept up by fashions or furies. No one can forget the seventeenth-century Dutch adventure with tulip bulbs or the South Seas Bubble of 1720, which attracted money from dukes and duchesses, princes and many ordinary folk, and then collapsed. There were railroad bubbles in the nineteenth century in which promoters would pump out stock as fast as money came in, diluting whatever early investors thought they might get. The late nineteenth century had mining stock scandals culminating in the demand that silver be made the backing for all American money. That did not happen. There were more than a few global stock scandals in the twentieth century — think of 1929 and of hot stock fashions that saw new technologies produce soaring stocks like instant-picture maker Polaroid Corp. It went bankrupt in 2001, was restructured, then went bankrupt again in 2008. The last decade of the twentieth century witnessed shocks in 1991, 1998, and the dot-com meltdown just as the twenty-first century began. And who can forget 2008–2009, when banks loaded up with crummy mortgages collapsed and nearly took down the world financial system.

We need a lesson from all this: Folks who put their money into assets they do not understand, whether commodities or tricky bonds or dubious stocks, stock funds or trends, hot Chinese banks or booming emerging markets, are lured by recent performance. The risk is the pistol to the investor's head. The bullet is everything he or she does not know.

HOW TO BUY BONDS

Now let's talk about the nuts and bolts of buying bonds. First, the rationale. Bonds have returned a few percent less than stocks over very long periods. For the 210 ten years from 1802 to 2012, stocks had a real (that is, inflation-adjusted) return of 6.6 percent per year.[2] In that 210 years, bonds' return was 3.6 percent after inflation. So stocks returned, one can say, nearly twice as much as bonds. Yet for some periods, for example, 1983 to 2015, bonds had an extraordinary run, generating returns averaging 8 percent per year.[3] In that period, stocks went through the flash crash of 1983, the dot-com meltdown, and the entire market implosion in 2008–2009, the latter driven in part by a form of bonds, mortgage backed securities with the characteristics of junk debt.

The 1983 to 2016 run of bonds was based on back-to-back processes. The U.S. Federal Reserve, directed by Paul Volcker, worked to break the back of double-digit inflation by forcing interest rates up, and then, with inflation under control, rates fell gradually and steadily to the year 2000. The Bank of Canada under Governor Gerald Bouey followed much the same course. In 2008 and 2009, central banks in the U.S., Canada, and Britain and the European Central Banks bought government and even some corporate bonds from banks to boost their cash positions and, as well, to drive down interest rates. It worked. Getting even 3 percent on a long government bond took a miracle or a genius. Rates remain in the low single digits. So why bother with bonds? Given that over average one-year periods, stocks outperform bonds 58.8 percent of the time, and for thirty years, do so 99.3 percent of the time, why would anyone invest in bonds?[4]

It's not to make a living. Rather, bonds in a portfolio can be regarded as insurance. If stocks crumble, it is a fairly sure bet that bonds will rise. Given that bonds do pay some return in the form of both interest and, often, capital gains if they are purchased right, bonds can be regarded as portfolio insurance that pays some of its cost.

Now let's look at the mechanics of bond buying. Once upon a time, there were Canada Savings Bonds. They paid relatively little — almost always less than what chartered banks and credit unions paid on savings — but they were obligations of the Government of Canada and as bulletproof as anything could be. If you lost a bond, the Bank of Canada would replace it — after a good deal of paperwork, including making a solemn promise in a written indemnity that if the lost bond turned up, you would not try to get paid for both. Public interest in CSBs waned with the paltry interest they paid. Toward the end of their life, as a way for the Government of Canada to raise money, regular CSBs paid 0.5 percent per year and the so-called premium CSBs paid 0.7 percent per year.

That was as much as short Government of Canada bonds paid for much of the time the issues were afloat, but lousy all the same. They encouraged those afraid of bank failure — the folks who preferred to stuff money in mattresses — to make loans for cheap to the same government that kept interest rates it would have to pay in the bargain basement. CSB sales ended in November 2017.

> If they are purchased right, bonds can be regarded as portfolio insurance that pays some of its cost.

If you want to hold real government bonds, you can buy them through an investment dealer, through an online discount brokerage, in bond mutual funds, or via packages of bonds in exchange traded funds. There is a vast choice of bonds to be had in ETFs, from shorts to longs and in Real Return Bonds (called Treasury Inflation Protected Securities in the U.S.), which adjust their value and price with changes in inflation rather than interest rates. The more efficient way to buy bonds for the average investor is to use a broad index such as the iShares Core Canadian Universe Bond Index ETF, symbol XBB, with a management expense ratio of 0.09 percent, which is 9/100ths of 1 percent. The cost of purchase is extra, but with online brokers it can be very low. The iShares 1- to 5-year laddered corporate bond ETF has a management fee of 28/100ths of 1 percent. As interest rates rise, the ladder will tend to generate more income. The downside of all bond ETFs, however, is that they never mature. In a worst case, which is hard to conceive, of runaway interest rates, as in the early 1980s when banks paid 15 percent annual interest on savings accounts, the ladders would not keep up and, as would be the case with all bond ETFs, holders could not take comfort in the eventual maturation of their bonds at 100 percent of face value.

The U.S. Treasury makes it possible to buy bonds directly. The program, called Treasury Direct, is described at treasurydirect.gov/indiv/products/products.htm. Those who wish to participate need a U.S. Social Security number or taxpayer ID documents, which are docu-ments issued by the Internal Revenue Service and the Social Security Administration. A document, called a TIN for Taxpayer Identification Number, puts holders into the U.S. tax world, for better and for worse. The Treasury Direct program is cost efficient and allows participants to join Treasury auctions and to access U.S. debt obligations for about the same price or cost on any given auction as Goldman Sachs pays. The downside is that participants in Canada or other foreign countries may wind up with U.S. tax and other compliance duties and costs.

If you want more yield than U.S. Treasuries or Government of Canada bonds can provide, you can go to supranational bonds issued by the World Bank. They have almost no default risk and so carry the credit ratings of very strong investment-grade bonds.

Then come Canadian provincial bonds and municipal bonds. The odds of a default are slight, for the provinces can tax, and if any province were thought close to default, other provinces and the federal government would rush to the rescue lest all provincial bonds be tainted and borrowing costs raised. At least that is the theory. No province has been close to default since the end of World War II, and the theory has not had to be tested. Provincial bonds are quite liquid and carry yield premiums over Government of Canada bonds of a fifth to half a percent. With ten-year federal bonds paying just a couple of percent at the time of writing, that little boost is valuable.

Canadian municipal bonds are riskier and yield more. Some are issued through provincial agencies that market the bonds, but these muni bonds are often hard to sell and even hard to track. We'd suggest staying away. The issue is liquidity and visibility. Lack of those virtues makes any asset worth less.

Corporate bonds vary, from top credits like BCE Inc. and the Royal Bank down to stuff issued by companies you've never heard of. You can sell BCE Inc. or Telus bonds, or bonds from Scotiabank or the Bank of Montreal, without too much trouble. Beware the little names, for these may be one-way bonds — easy to buy, almost impossible to sell, and hard to price. In the bond biz, all trades are over the counter. There is no single central board like that for stocks listed in Toronto or New York, Paris or London. Trading bonds already on the market can require patience to get a bid and the understanding that the guy with $1 million of a federal bond to trade is going to get a better price than a person with $10,000 to trade. Bonds have a place in many portfolios, but many investors go the easy route of leaving trading and management to bond mutual funds or exchange traded funds. With a decent record and fees well below 1 percent, it's often the wise thing to do.

> Beware the little names, for these may be one-way bonds — easy to buy, almost impossible to sell, and hard to price.

If you want to buy single corporate bonds, you have to do a lot of research. Check ratings at DBRS or Moody's or S&P. Ask a broker or online dealer research department for a report. Read the bond covenants, which establish the rules of each bond, say what creditor rights are, explain risks, and discuss recourse for nonpayment. Some bonds have been issued with covenants that declare holders have no rights other than to be paid. Other bonds are convertible to stocks and have elaborate explanations of conversion premiums.

All credit ratings are based on event risk; that is, some chance or some reason a bond may default or that the borrower may have problems if this or that event or process occurs. Conventional bonds have interest rate risk, for if rates rise, existing bonds will be less attractive at their face rates and may, therefore, lose market price until they approach maturity and offer return of their face value.

Other bonds called "linkers" set the bond's payout based on inflation rates. As inflation rises, bonds like Canada's Real Return Bonds (RRBs) and American Treasury Inflation-Protected Securities (TIPS) raise their payouts. Whether a conventional bond or a linker is a good deal involves comparing the base payout of some percentage and your own forecast for inflation. Holding some linkers for inflation insurance is not unwise, but most linkers have an implicit charge for the inflation protection they provide and thus pay less than a conventional bond. There are TIPS and RRB exchange traded funds that provide liquidity, immediate pricing, and diversification, usually at a low cost. As well, there are some mutual funds with a reputation for wise management of RRBs. Seek and ye shall find.

BOND RATINGS

Rating agencies — Moody's Investors Service, Standard & Poor's, Fitch, and the Canadian rater known as DBRS — make a living judging the credit worthiness of national governments and corporations that issue bonds. The ratings are finely tuned, from AAA, which means the issuer has an extremely strong capacity to service the bonds and pay interest; to single A minus, which means strong but not extremely strong; to BBB plus, which means adequate capacity to pay interest; to B minus, which means vulnerable to changing business conditions; to the C range, which means vulnerable; down to D, which means the issuer has defaulted on one or more coupon payments.

Bonds rated A almost never default; corporate Bs default 10 percent to 30 percent of the time, depending on how closely one distills the ratings; and corporate Cs default as much as 69 percent of the time before maturity. Note that all government bonds have better odds of payment than corporate bonds because even if subnational governments can't mint money, they can collect taxes to pay their debts. Bonds rated BBB- or higher by Standard & Poor's are considered investment grade. AAA corporate bonds are very rare. In the U.S., for example, only Microsoft Inc. and Johnson & Johnson have this elite rating among corporate issuers. For peace of mind, AAA and A ratings are worth having. For a fairly routine investment, bonds with A ratings and ten years or less to go before redemption tend to be fairly safe bets. Nothing is for sure, of course.

JUNK BONDS

Below investment grade, the vast field of bonds that should but — who knows? — may not pay interest are considered junk. They may have low ratings or not be rated at all. They pay more, they rise and fall in price with issuers' financial conditions, and they are a field and market of their own. At one time — that's before 1970 — junk bonds were untradeable. Moreover, any company that could not get a decent rating for a bond — that would be in the Bs or better — could not sell them.

Junk bonds became saleable and tradeable through the efforts of U.S. financier Michael Milken who, for those efforts and many technical violations of U.S. securities laws, served twenty-two months in U.S. federal custody. His personal compensation for creating and often micromanaging the junk bond market in the 1980s is said to have exceeded US$1 billion, then a record sum. His defence to many charges was that his opponents, including federal prosecutors, did not understand relevant securities laws as well as he did. Indeed, bad karma and sheer ego were intrinsic to his downfall. His employer, Drexel Burnham Lambert, a respected brokerage, collapsed. A multi-billionaire, Milken has left the legacy of a vigorous junk bond market. He funds medical research on a large scale and in finance is regarded as a sage, though formally banned from the securities industry.

> Leave junk to the professionals or use an ETF — the risks of riding in this roller-coastering asset class are daunting.

Today, junk bonds are a legitimate field of investment. They are highly volatile and, as a group, vary in price so much that they can yield 200 basis points more than U.S. Treasury ten-year bonds, or as much as 1,200 basis points when the economy is in a shambles and corporate finances are in the dog house.

For any individual investor, junk bonds are a bad idea. They are hard to trade in an illiquid market and require intense research before purchase. Junk rated in the C level has cumulative default rates of 69 percent.

The case for junk is not closed, however. There are professional managers, such as Toronto-based Marret Asset Management Inc., that manage these bonds. The investor who wants into this market should use a high-yield bond ETF such as the iShares High Yield Bond Index ETF hedged to the Canadian dollar, which has a 4.1 percent average annual yield for the five years ended June 30, 2018. In short, leave junk to the professionals or use an ETF. In any event, junk should be a small part of your portfolio. The risks of riding in this roller-coastering asset class are daunting.

BONDS THAT DON'T PAY INTEREST

What use is a bond that pays no annual or semi-annual interest? Such critters exist. They are called strips in Canada, from the idea that a single coupon is sliced off and sold for a price that should be the present discounted value; that is, what sum at today's interest rate will rise to in future at the date of maturity of the coupon. In the U.S., these are called zeros; that is, zero coupon bonds held for a future payoff.

A variant of the zero/strip was employed by Ottawa office tower builder Robert Campeau in a series of takeovers of American retail giants like Federated Department Stores. Using leveraged buyouts financed by bonds invented by the late legendary takeover artist and lawyer Bruce Wasserstein, a man of superb credentials (Harvard Law, University of Cambridge, then the ultra-patrician law firm Cravath, Swaine & Moore) and predatory instincts, Campeau Corporation issued a variant of the zero, the Pay in Kind bond, which provided no cash interest on what was speculative junk. Instead, the PIKs paid junk and the whole affair collapsed with the bankruptcies of Federated and Allied department store chains, which controlled Macy's and Bloomingdale and about 250 other American retailers. Wrote the *New York Times* of the process, "Any corporate executive can figure out how to file for bankruptcy when the bottom drops out of the business. It took the special genius of Robert Campeau, chairman of the Campeau Corporation, to figure out how to bankrupt more than 250 profitable department stores. The dramatic jolt to Bloomingdale's, Abraham & Straus, Jordan Marsh and the other proud stores reflects his overreaching grasp and oversized ego."[5] Eventually Campeau left Canada for Austria, then his wife left him or the other way around, he sued her for support since he had given her all his money, he slunk back to Canada, and then he checked out of life altogether in June 2017 at the age of ninety-three.

The Campeau gigaflop has several lessons for ordinary investors:

- Don't buy any bond that does not pay current interest.
- Buy strips or zeros only if you want to park money to be used in a certain year, such as when a child starts university. With no current interest, these bonds tend to be extra risky. They

will gyrate in price like the long bonds they are. A ten-year strip will drop 10 percent in value for every 1 percent rise in market interest. A thirty-year strip will rise by 30 percent if market interest rates drop by 1 percent. Don't buy corporate bonds that finance fancy deals if you don't understand the deals. Bond risk rises with time to repayment. This fact is fundamental to investing in bonds. And corporate credit risk only adds to what may happen, usually on the downside.

> Bond risk rises with time to repayment — this fact is fundamental to investing in bonds.

- If the issuer of a bond can't afford to pay semi-annual or annual cash interest on a bond, you are nuts to buy it.

- For any bond, look to the reasons it is being sold, where the money raised will wind up, and, most of all, the character of the people running the show. Screwball projects and enterprises that will be built on air by people with dark pasts or ominous presents should be avoided. The foundation of capital markets has to be honesty. If it is not there, don't venture.

SYNTHETIC BONDS

Investment bankers have been nothing if not inventive when it comes to creating bonds out of other bonds. In the 1990s, as interest rates were dropping, big stock brokers went to work on existing government and high-grade corporate bonds, slicing off the coupons and the principal — this was done figuratively, given that bonds are now mostly just book entries without paper certificates — and brewing the pot of interest to pay more per year for fewer years, less, of course, fees for doing the job. The new bonds, cleverly named after carnivorous animals, were derivatives built on other assets' income streams. The critters bore costs to investors, for investment bankers, after all, need to be paid.

The moral of this story is that, as the cliché goes, there is no free lunch. If someone offers you a government bond with an interest rate well above the going rate, look under the covers. There has to be someone stirring the cauldron and cackling all the way to his or her bank.

NVCCS

The 2008 to 2009 global banking crisis forced governments around the world to act as lenders or guarantors of crumbled banks. They were insolvent, for the banks' liabilities exceeded their assets, often because the assets, the loans and fancy credit structures, were out of money — bankrupt, to use the broader term. Global financial authorities and, in particular, the Bank for International Settlements in Basel, Switzerland, effectively the central bank for the world's central banks, created a new concept, the Non-Viability Contingent Capital bond, which would, under specified conditions, turn into common stock. That means that the bank issuing the NVCCs did not have to pay interest or give the money back if the trigger were pulled and the bond turned into equity. The NVCC was born.[6]

Canadian chartered banks issue NVCCs with interest rates higher than those of their usual bonds, which must have interest paid and capital refunded at maturity no matter what. The NVCCs are often less liquid than conventional bonds, carry more risk, and would turn into the common stock of effectively bankrupt banks at the worst time imaginable. Large investors use NVCCs in order to get more bang for their buck. As of the time of writing, NVCCs are expected to go into major bond indexes. That will make them more visible and more liquid. You can buy them if you think that a big chartered bank will never be insolvent. Trouble is, back in 2008, many banks in Europe, the U.S., and the Far East were technically insolvent. It could happen again. NVCC holders would then have common stock, probably with no dividends, priced probably near zero. It would be just about worthless paper from worthless banks.

Should ordinary investors, the civilians of the bond market, invest in synthetic bonds and NVCCs? We think not. If you want equity or other risk, then buy stock. If you want the security of a bond, liquidity, and certainty of what it is worth now and at maturity, buy the conventional government bond or investment-grade corporate bond.

ASSET-BACKED SECURITIES (ABS)

There are good bonds and surely there are bad bonds, but the worst of the worst turned out to be collateralized debt obligations. CDOs were flows of interest payments structured in layers to provide all cash flow from the whole shebang to the top layer or tranche (French for slice), then to lower layers as cash came in. CDOs, which were mostly American, were built usually of crappy mortgages and sometimes of auto loans and even credit card loans. The way they worked is as follows:

Take several thousand dubious mortgages and strip every interest payment off one by one. Pile 'em up. You will have a heap — call it a pyramid — which you slice into, say, thirty-six layers. The top layer gets all the money coming in until the owners of the tranche are paid, then the money goes to the next layer, then the next, and so on. The top layers are almost sure to get paid; the next is a pretty sure thing, too. Go down to the middle layer and there is a good chance of some defaults. Down at the bottom layers, the odds of full and even partial payment are dim.

Top layers of CDOs sold for prices that indicated expectation of full payment. They were synthetic bonds but with pedigrees. The interest rates were consistent with mid to high levels of investment-grade corporate debt. In the middle, the interest rose to levels consistent with junk bonds. At the bottom, promises of 36 percent interest, unthinkable for real bonds even when government bonds fetched 8 percent, indicated that holders had as much chance of getting paid as a monkey typing *Romeo and Juliet* on the first try. No wonder the bottom layers were called "toxic waste." Nobody wanted them. What to do?

Investment bankers — taking a leaf from the book of famed American bank robber Willie Sutton, who is said to have quipped about his targets, "I rob 'em because that's where the money is" — combined toxic waste from many CDOs and made what were called CDOs squared; that is, CDO^2. Then that toxic waste was turned into CDOs cubed; that is, CDO^3.

Amazingly, some credit rating agencies said this stuff would work, and sometimes it did. The holders were usually playing Russian roulette if they held anything but the top layers of the first CDOs. It was an American disaster. In Canada, a variant, ABCP, or asset-backed commercial paper, was rated by only one agency. The big global bond raters would not touch it.

The savants of Wall Street called the CDOs "potentially lethal," to use Warren Buffett's language. Another wit called them "a tangled hairball of risk." In the end, some players made money, especially investment bankers who had found a way to pawn off NINJA (No Income, No Job, No other Assets) loans. Most investors in the CDOs were wiped out.

Recently, CDOs have made a comeback as asset-backed securities, this time with credit card payments. The riskiest notes backed by credit card loans yield about 2.3 percent more than Government of Canada bonds. That's a good boost, but if the default rate exceeds 2.3 percent, the investor is bathing in red ink. Better quality debt from large corporations yields about 1.5 percent to 2.5 percent more than Canada bonds of similar term.

> The savants of Wall Street called CDOs "potentially lethal," while another wit called them "a tangled hairball of risk."

We need not dissect the twists and turns of these synthetic bonds, save to say that the lesson is always buy what you understand, keep it simple, and if the story is long and the deals contingent on a chain of payoffs, walk away. Bottom line: Given that bonds are supposed to be safer than stocks, stick to the real thing.

CONVERTIBLES

Convertible bonds are a species of their own. The concept is a bond with an option to turn the debt into equity. The packaging is often done to make lower grade bonds appeal to investors who are willing to take on more risk in exchange for lower interest than might be paid on a straight bond. If the company issuing the convertible just lumbers along and does not raise its earnings, the bond will be paid at a decent rate of interest on its face or as bought in the market, and, if the company thrives, the bond can be turned into stock at a defined exercise price.

The mechanics of convertible bonds are simple in principle but often daunting in practice. The basics are straightforward. The bond has a conversion premium. It is the difference between the price on the market or what you may pay and the price that the bond might sell for without the conversion feature. It is like an option that allows the bond holder to turn the asset into stock. If the stock rises above the conversion price, it is said to be "in the money."

There is a fallback provision on convertibles, for the issuer usually has the right after a set number of years to call (take back or cancel) the conversion feature by paying a predetermined premium. For example, if the bond has a four-year grace period before the issue can call it and the trigger is that the stock trades, say, at 45 percent over the conversion price for a month (a frequent condition), then the issuer can call it after giving notice.

Convertibles make sense for the long-term investor who wants downside price protection on stock and a shot at capital gains if the issuer does well. The problem is that convertibles require a good deal of calculation: they need yield calculations to compare what the bond yields versus the stock's dividend yield, then a calculation of the convertible's premium at the conversion ratio when the bond turns into stock, then a comparison of the premium the bond carries as a conversion option, and all of that in relation to the yield advantage. Even then, you have to evaluate the value of conversion over the time to when the bond may be called. If this sounds complex, it is. It is often easier to buy both the bond, because you like the yield in relation to the safety or rating, and the stock, because you think well of the company's prospects. The old phrase "There ain't no such thing as a free lunch" applies here, if you ignore the double negative.

PREFERRED STOCKS

Preferred stocks offer a fixed dividend or a dividend paid according to a formula; for example, 3 percent over the five-year Treasury bond rate. They tend to be recallable at the wish of the issuer. Superficially, the guarantee of some rate of dividend plus the dividend tax credit, which reduces tax payable on stock dividends, makes them more appealing to some investors than the bonds of the same company.

But there are big differences. Bond holders must be paid or they can put the deadbeat company into bankruptcy. Preferred stockholders only have the privilege of being paid before any common stockholders can be paid. Worse, preferred shares often come with a covenant; that is, a contractual condition that allows the issuer to call in the shares if interest rates rise. At the same time, the issuer may lower the dividend if interest rates fall. It's a "heads I win, tails you lose" deal and, in spite of what seem to be solid fundamentals, preferred stocks remain mostly a retail product structured to appeal to small investors.

One of Canada's most savvy professional investors, James Hymas, runs $30 million of preferreds under the umbrella of Hymas Investment Management Inc. in Toronto. He squeezes substantial gains out of preferreds with fast trading and a great deal of insight into what many regard as a justly ignored hybrid of stocks and bonds.

Preferred stocks are specialty investments, more so than generic government bonds or straight corporate bonds. Yet there are some specialized preferreds that are issued by Canadian companies and that pay in U.S. dollars. Two large energy companies, Alta Gas and Enbridge, for example, have such preferreds. To be sure, there are many common stocks listed in Canada that also pay dividends in U.S. dollars.

Hymas is sanguine about the ability of issuers to call in issues of preferreds just as rising interest rates can make them much more appealing. "An investor has to understand the purchase and the tradeoff," he explains. That's true for any investment, but especially true for this "kinda bond, kinda stock" flavour of fixed income.

THE PROBLEM OF TRADING BONDS

Trading bonds isn't as easy as it used to be. Chartered banks used to be major bond dealers, but they have become shy of holding bonds in inventory to sell to interested clients or buying bonds from clients to add to their shelf inventory. They do carry inventories of government bonds and big issues of corporate bonds, but those big issues, large in dollar value, are actually a fraction of all bonds outstanding. The big banks don't keep or trade small issues much. The reasons are structural and regulatory.

Structurally, the problem is that bonds are bought or sold by dealers who trade them on their own account in what is largely an over-the-counter market in which buyer and seller strike a bargain often invisible to the larger market. The traders are guided by bond boards that post trades in a relatively small number of large bond issues of fairly well-known companies or governments. But the comprehensive price and volume data on major stock exchanges does not exist for bonds. Ironically, the value of bonds outstanding far exceeds that of stocks — though nobody actually knows how many bonds and of what value they are. Small issues of smallish companies that are sold and seldom traded disappear from view.

Stocks, however, are traded by dealers as agents. As bond owners, banks and other bond dealers care very much about the trade price and they want to make hefty profits. As stock trading agents, on the other hand, the commission is enough and depends little or not at all on the price of a trade. The consequence of all this is that banks, when trading bonds, own them for a time and have to accept the risks of default or market price wobble. That puts their capital at risk.

> Ironically, the value of bonds outstanding far exceeds that of stocks — though nobody actually knows how many bonds and of what value they are.

You might say that a couple of hundredths of 1 percent, which is what bond dealers make when trading with insurance companies and other large institutions, should not matter. Yet in the financial crisis of 2008 to 2009, when bond markets seized up and there were no bids for lots of corporate bonds, banks got stuck. They held bonds of companies that were good credits one day and insolvent the next. The banks had to write down their capital held to back the bonds in their inventory, especially in Europe, where in some countries — think of Cyprus, where there were huge loans, dicey bonds as collateral, and very dicey customers who wanted their money laundered — banks were left with more liabilities than assets. The banks were bust. It was the Greek mess of national debts that could not be paid by tax collections and an economy that could not support more tax collections. It resembled the Irish mess, in which the national government bailed out two large banks and wound up with rotten loans on overpriced real estate developments that could not be sold, although the Greek situation was exponentially worse. International banking regulators and many national banking authorities working through the Bank for International Settlements decided that if banks as bond dealers want to hold corporate bonds and even many kinds of government bonds as inventory or trading with clients, they would have to add capital. That immobilizes money and cuts bank earnings that are in large part derived from how much leverage banks can get out of their capital.

Long story short: Banks decided to cut their participation in the bond market. Customers who used to be able to flip XYZ corporation's ten-year bonds or five-year notes, ninety-day bills, and much more found that the banks either would not act as buyers or would not have inventory to sell. The result: Banks act as intermediaries and seek someone on the other side of a customer's wish to trade a certain bond. For government bonds, especially those recently issued and heavily traded, called "on the run" in the bond market, it's not a problem. For old bonds, especially corporate bonds issued in small batches under, say, $25 million, it is almost impossible to find counterparties without forcing the customer to sell for cheap or to pay dearly — a "wide spread" in securities trading lingo.

BOND FUNDS

Today, for the ordinary investor who wants bonds for such sound reasons as having an asset that tends to go up when stocks go down or having a very well-defined and very certain flow of cash, owning actual bonds is inefficient. The trading costs are high. Dealers may not want to trade. And the complexities of corporate bonds — call dates when the issuers can cancel the bonds and refund their price, managing maturities, and reading covenants that vary from one bond to another — all call out for simplification.

And that simplification is bond mutual funds. Bond funds come in hundreds of flavours of risk, maturity, nationality, tracking interest rates or inflation, currencies, industries included or excluded, government groupings, and more. Bond mutual funds are an old idea — a smart manager assembles a portfolio of bonds and trades them in order to manage risk and return. The problem with bond mutual funds is that, for the investor with less than $100,000 for a bond fund investment or, sometimes, $100,000 for all investments with a particular mutual fund management company — the limits are quite variable — the fees, typically 1 percent to as much as 2 percent in balanced funds holding bonds, severely limit the returns the investor can expect or will receive. In these funds, there is little left for the investor after fees are charged.

Some managers are wise, some are not, but given the basically low interest rates of all bonds these days, the management fees are heavy weights to carry. Some bond funds come with guarantees of return of 80 percent of money invested no matter what. These are called segregated, or seg, funds, also available to cover common stock risk. The required hold period for the guarantee is ten years in most cases, and the seg fund insurance charge on top of the customary management expense ratio makes low-return bond packages nearly useless. But there is qualification. Had you bought a common stock seg fund in 1998 or 1999, the wretched collapse of 2008 would have been a small matter. Your losses would have been limited. It is harder to justify any bond seg fund, for, from a very long point of view, the bond bull is still running or at least limping. It is not possible to say that bond prices will not one day collapse, as many did in the 1970s when interest rates soared and old bond prices collapsed, but it seems remote from the perspective of 2018. Today's weak government bond prices reflect rising interest rates, but bonds still provide an anchor of value and promised return if held to maturity. They have a role as safety nets if not as hot speculations.

We need to consider whether managed bond funds are worthwhile. The jury is out on this one. There are, to be sure, some very able bond managers. Charging a lot for genius management on a stock fund with an unbounded upper growth limit may be acceptable. On a bond fund with a limited upside, it is not. Worse, on money market funds that hold treasury bills and other fairly liquid assets, management fees may leave little for the fund investor. Just as an example, the RBC Canadian Money Market Fund Series A had an average annual return for the ten years ended June 30, 2018, of 0.6 percent. The fund's management expense ratio is 0.6 percent. That is the same as the return for the decade. The top investments ranked by size in the portfolio are short corporate notes mostly issued by other chartered banks. One could say that money market funds have had their day. They offer scant returns not much more and often less than the fees paid for management. If you want bonds, either buy the real thing or use low-fee bond ETFs whose fees are much less than even paltry money market fund returns.

Bond exchange traded funds come in even more flavours and with much lower fees than most bond mutual funds offer. Take the Blackrock iShares collection of bond ETFs. There are 109 variations, from the basic iShares Core Canadian Universe Bond ETF with a management fee of just 9 basis points. It tracks the FTSE TMX Canada Universe Bond Index and is tradeable instantly with continuous pricing, as all ETFs have, every moment of the day that stock exchanges are open. There are corporate iShares variations, inflation-linked bonds, and ladders of bonds from one to ten years. Other vendors have comparable offerings. They are cheap, transparent, and almost completely immune to meddling by greedy traders, but they have one drawback — their holdings never mature. In our opinion, that is a small issue against so many advantages, but it does mean that there is no automatic refund of the bond's principal. The owner gives up the protection of refund of capital and must take on some responsibility for management. In our view, that's a good deal.

> Bond ETFs are cheap, transparent, and almost completely immune to meddling by greedy traders, but they have one drawback — their holdings never mature.

BOUQUETS OF BONDS

The idea of a bond — that the holder is entitled to be paid and, if not, can seize or sue assets of the deadbeat company or, for that matter, airport authority, shipping line, railroad, or nation — has flowered into many forms, many of which dilute the holder's rights. However, for each tiny turn to open the faucet of risk, the prospective yield of the bond rises.

We need to employ some common sense here. As bonds move in quality from sovereign bonds issued by nations that have the power to print money to abject junk that probably will default before maturity, risk rises from slight to astronomical. At some point, the safety of the bond, which is the core idea of the asset class, gets to be forgotten. These risky bonds are for specialists able to parse the idea of a bond with others willing to take the other side of the bet. Thus, the moral of the tale: Only buy bonds you understand. If you are dazzled by their complexity or bamboozled by the details, take our core advice — don't do it!

CHAPTER 5

Stocks: Sharing in Ownership and Risk

Many people have an opinion on stocks, but few understand the market that sets their prices. No investor can claim to understand the stock market in close detail, for problems and paradoxes come up and disappear like a game of whack-a-mole.

The first question is, why invest at all in stocks? They rise and fall at times like roller coasters, making some investors fortunes and wrecking others' bank accounts. The answer is that there is no other asset class that offers their combination of liquidity — so that you can buy or sell at any moment during the business day or even at holiday midnights on some global exchanges — price visibility, low trading costs, and potential for gain. Yes, the risk is there. But as you'll see, it is manageable. Most of all, stock portfolios can be fine-tuned with far less capital at stake than is needed to assemble a portfolio of real estate or a deck of bonds with desired terms and yields. To pick a sum, $100,000 can buy a handsome clutch of stocks.

There is chance in investing in anything and, for that matter, risk in investing in nothing. We all have future liabilities such as the cost of raising a family, buying a new car, and retiring. To the extent that earned, after-tax income does not cover all these things, one needs to build a financial reserve. All that is obvious. But why use stocks, which, as everyone knows, have the unhappy tendency to plummet just at the wrong moments?

Stocks have special qualities that other assets lack. As we note in other chapters of *Cherished Fortune*, you can invest in land or bonds, or, for that matter you can leave your money in a bank to grow slowly with interest. Each alternative lacks at least one quality of stocks. Land is illiquid. Bonds other than fresh government issues take time to trade and often have such wide spreads between bid and ask that a positive return is hard to achieve. Ephemeral investments like baseball cards and even serious art are traded in markets controlled by dealers or in auctions with huge fees to buyer and seller that typically total 25 percent of the gavel price. With stocks, the price is the same for one share or ten or a hundred or a thousand. No other asset class matches that kind of financial democracy. At any second, the price of shares of the Royal Bank or any other company listed on a stock exchange are the same for somebody who wants to pick up a hundred or a fund manager who has to bag 100,000.

> With stocks, the price is the same for one share or a thousand. No other asset class matches that kind of democracy.

With all of that said, where do you start? A small hardware store cannot instantly become Home Depot, but — and this is the key — it can serve a small neighbourhood or a small part of the hardware and paint business very well. A store selling antique door hardware and elaborate wrought iron screens can thrive if major stores do not stock such things. There are niches in hardware and often in stocks. The treasure hunt goes to investors who can identify bargains or who have the tenacity and, perhaps, wisdom, to be patient.

WHERE TO START

We need some ground rules for investing in stocks and, for that matter, other assets, too. First, make sure time is on your side. In other words, you have to be able to wait out the peaks and valleys of price fluctuations. The more you extend time, the more these peaks and valleys lose their importance. This view takes persistence and faith, not blindness.

Second, understand your asset space. Exposure to stocks is really exposure to economic growth. Stocks vary in their quality and risk, but their fate is inevitably tied to the larger economy. Never lose sight of the big picture. Some stocks race ahead of the economy, but most are eventually brought to earth or even raised from the depths of despair by major economic trends.

Third, know the top line — that is, what the company does and the long-term history and prospect for sales. The prospective investment should be growing in a thriving business. Today, online retailing is thriving. Amazon.com Inc. had 2017 sales of US$177.9 billion compared to US$61 billion in 2012. It is leaving many conventional brick-and-mortar retailers in the dust or in bankruptcy. Point is, to put money into a dying industry just because the stock is cheap (and deservedly so) is foolish. So-called deep value investors invest money in stocks that are very cheap by almost every measure, figuring that they are getting a huge bargain. Stock markets are efficient over the long run as investors, especially big institutions like pension funds, shop for good places to put their money and sell what isn't going to thrive. In small cap space — that is, little stocks for which the market is not necessarily efficient — bargains are offered from time to time. But those bargains call for research skills. Like diving into deep water, it's only a good idea for those who know how to swim.

Fourth, diversify. Inexperienced investors often plunge, putting all or almost all of their savings into one thing. That is the path to disaster. Nortel Networks is the most famous recent giant Canadian collapse, taking down a third of the Toronto Stock Exchange. In the U.S. there is no lack of failure. Recently, General Electric slashed its dividend by half, as it did twice before during economic crises.[1] In June 2018, it suffered the indignity of being dropped from the Dow Jones Industrial Average, where it had been listed since 1896. Have faith in the process, but not in any one company or even industry.

SO MANY STOCKS, SO LITTLE TIME

The stock universe — that is, the number of companies whose shares can be bought or sold — is measured in the tens of thousands. As of the end of 2016, there were over 3,400 listings on the Toronto Stock Exchange, while the New York Stock Exchange had 2,300 active names. The NASDAQ had another 2,900. Then there are European markets, Australian markets, Asian markets, and markets in some developing countries. For example, Kazakhstan has had a stock market since 1993, Uzbekistan since 1994. Where do you start hunting for shares?

For an individual investor, the problem is daunting, not just to pick which of many banks to buy, which of many railroads, et cetera, but how much of each and at what price any shares are attractive.

INVESTMENT FUNDS

Investment funds are a place to start. Managed mutual funds hire experts to do the allocating and trading. The fees tend to be in the range of 1 percent to 3 percent depending on the fund, type of asset, how much service and handholding is provided by advisors selling the funds, advertising cost, and record of management. Mutual funds, formerly called investment trusts, offer a measure of expertise, but at several not well recognized costs. First, the fees stock mutual funds charge in Canada, one of the most expensive places in the world to own a mutual fund, average 2.6 percent a year plus GST. If you buy with so-called deferred sales commission, which sticks you with a 5 percent to 6 percent penalty if you sell out more than 10 percent of your position in the first year or two, and a little less or perhaps no penalty after six years have elapsed from purchase, the fees are very expensive. The little 2.6 percent charge adds up to 26 percent if you hold for ten years and 52 percent if you hold for twenty years. Growth of assets masks this charge, but it is nevertheless a huge headwind when you compare a mutual fund with its benchmark.

Investing in pure benchmarks is a perfectly valid thing to do via ETFs. There is a scholarly literature which argues that managers cannot beat pure index investing over time. Discovered or recognized by

Burton Malkiel, a distinguished economist at Princeton University, it works for the U.S. market, but not for others. Reason: No other national stock market is so diversified, so able to fix one company's crummy performance or even one sector's bad year with some other company or industry that had a great year. Moreover, tweaks to the U.S. indices via rules-based stock selection, a process called "smart beta" for the second letter of the Greek alphabet, which represents relative volatility in the securities biz, seems to add little value in the U.S. It adds a lot of value in other national markets.

Mutual funds offer a measure of expertise, but at several not well recognized costs.

Managed index funds seek alpha, which is performance over an index with beta, but have mixed results achieving that goal. As for attempts to beat the averages, we have to give a qualified answer. For markets outside the huge U.S. stock market, lack of diversification (as in Canada), smallness of the market (as in many emerging nations), lack of dependable information (once again, as in many emerging markets), and even uninvestable indexes (as in some developing markets) make the Malkiel concept of the superiority of index investing variously invalid, unworkable, or undependable. Add currency conversion issues, such as getting a good price going in and out of little-traded currencies, and the winner often comes out as the managed fund run by people who know the score in faraway lands.

That does not mean that managed funds are a consistent solution. Part of the problem is that a mutual fund ought to be a simple concept but is no such thing. Portfolios change, which is expected. Mandates to do this or that change. The indices they follow may change and provide incentives to managers to change their strategies. And managers may change, the new tossing out the duds of the old.

Worse, managed funds may have a lot of turnover caused by managers' changing ideas of which stocks to trade. In a tough year when market averages are falling and unitholders want their money back, the stock winners, which have run up gains, may be sold. That happened in 2008, when every asset class, including many kinds of corporate and mid to long government bonds, went into forced sales to raise cash. Mutual funds were down severely in 2008, as were global stock markets, but, worse, forced sales by mutual fund unitholders generated big income tax liabilities for anyone who did not hold units within RRSPs. (There were no TFSAs to shelter stocks or other financial assets until January 1, 2009.) Finally, for all their advertising, glitz, and testimonials about how they can finance retirements and growth charts (with the little caution that "past perform-ance cannot predict future performance)," many mutual funds are what the securities business calls "index huggers"; that is, they are little different from their benchmarks.

In Canada, a small financial market, some of the hugging problem is inevitable. If a fund is mandated to hold large caps, the big banks, some big oils, maybe a big gold miner, and some railroad shares are inevitable. Managers who want to avoid getting fired for underperform-ance structure their funds to resemble the benchmark. They may, for example, have a little less telecom and a little more insurance, but they are closet index funds sold with high fees. If the fund is mandated to hold Government of Canada long bonds, the manager has almost no discretion. They will have a load of qualifying bonds with maturities of ten to thirty years with yields clustering with 25 to 35 basis points over the ten-year yield. Some funds do better than others chiefly because they have more money to lever down trading fees by a couple of hun-dredths of one percent or because they charge clients less. But they will not beat their indices

When there is room for a manager to manoeuvre, things change. Midcap and small cap funds give mutual fund managers more room to be creative, and, indeed, many management companies do well in this space.[2]

Finally, we come to the philosophical question: What is the right index? For a plain stock fund, say U.S. large caps, the S&P 500 is fine. How about a capped version that limits the holdings to a given level? Not quite the same thing, but okay given that most mutual funds have a 10 percent cap on any one company. But when a mutual fund man-dates that it will hold a certain percentage of Canadian stocks and has an allowance for U.S. or foreign stocks, then the indices will have to be tailored to fit. If the index then mirrors the fund's structure, it can only be used to compare what is in the fund to the tailored index. It is a mirror, not a standard anymore.

An alternative is the concept of the exchange traded stock fund. There are perhaps 30,000 ETFs operating, with dozens more starting up every week. Picking one or two is itself as challenging as the problem of picking stocks. ETFs that are capitalization weighted — that is, loaded with shares priced by each component's share price multiplied by the number of shares on the market — tend to be top heavy with recent hot performers. Apple Inc., for example, is 10 percent of the American S&P 500 Index. Loaded with recent winners, raw index funds offer the opportunity to buy high, and the investor may, in the event of a crash, wind up selling low.

ETFs based on major averages are something like agnostics in church. The ETFs that replicate the largest U.S. stocks, say the S&P 500, have both recent winners and recent losers. The American economy is diversified like no other, so the S&P 500 ETFs fulfill the concept of diversification quite well. But the Canadian broad market ETFs that replicate the TSX are far less diversified. They are overloaded with banks, which are leveraged lenders subject to damage if interest rates are not properly managed by the Bank of Canada, and packed with energy producers that are in a slump because of low global oil prices.

One solution is to use equally weighted ETFs so that every company's shares have equal influence on price and performance. In the S&P 500 index of the biggest 500 American public company, the biggest companies' shares and the smallest have equal weight. There is more room for the little guys to grow and less chance for big guys like Nortel Networks, the most famous flop of a Canadian large cap, and once a third of the TSX by weight, to wipe out investors.

The virtue of buying ETFs is that they provide diversification, thus lowering the risks of stock selection. Moreover, their fees are low, some as little as 7/100ths of 1 percent of shares in the ETFs, so that one can afford to hold through many ups and downs. They reduce risk over long periods, though with virtually no cash in their accounts they are pure market risk. Some mutual funds, on the other hand, have a good deal of cash. That slows the ascent of funds because cash tends to earn little, but cash is a cushion on the way down. In this sense, mutual funds can be less risky than ETFs with identical holdings.

Over long periods, broadly focused ETFs have tended to outperform mutual funds with similar or even identical assets. Part of the reason is the fee drag of mutual funds and part is the inability of managers of conventional mutual funds to predict the future. Ordinary index-following ETFs with broad market mandates for large markets such as the Russell 5000, which pretty well covers the listed stocks in America, tend to beat managers because their fees are low and because nobody, not any quantitative investment guru nor complex option strategy meister, can deal with the mathematical problem of trying to optimize future returns of 500, much less 5,000, companies operating in different markets, some in different countries, currencies, technologies, and so on.

> The virtue of buying ETFs is that they provide diversification, thus lowering the risks of stock selection. Moreover, their fees are low.

There are mathematical "solutions" for all of this and there are computers that can do millions of calculations a second, but nobody has the inside track. Moreover, some index calculation rules exclude outliers, such as stocks that add 100 percent per week to their value, as Bitcoin did in 2017 and as some marijuana stocks seem to do each month. Those exclusions keep the indices "realistic," but they also do not reveal the gambling component of investing. Nevertheless, the larger the market and the more complex the structure and holdings, the more likely it is that a plain vanilla ETF with low fees and no theory at all will beat most if not all managers. And data show that of the managers who do come out on top, there is no persistence.[3] Why chase it? "Go ETF" is the way this argument ends.

Investors who buy into the idea of one size fits all can get balanced managed funds. This is the most agnostic approach of all. There are many hundreds of Canadian balanced funds, most with about 60 percent stocks and 40 percent bonds. The stocks tend to be issues from huge companies like banks, the bonds government five- or ten-year issues. These funds often produce large amounts of dividends and interest, which is not necessarily a good thing for investors who are fully taxable. There is often not much growth and a lot of tax exposure.

Investors can adjust their own ratios of stocks to bonds just by altering the ratio of stock funds to bond funds. That way, the one-size-fits-all management fee, which can be about 3 percent for stocks, does not squeeze blood out of bonds that barely return 3 percent. With growing understanding of stocks and fund managers who may be forced to sell stocks to raise cash for some investors, burdening all with taxable gains or losses that are unwanted or unneeded for taxable accounts, the investor can start to build a bespoke portfolio. Investors concerned with ethics can shed distillers or gun makers, buy more or fewer energy producers depending on outlook, buy companies that make products out of animal parts or reject them. Other investors will happily go overweight on banks or will reject banks as leveraged lenders at risk of interest rate spikes and loan defaults. Knowledge is the foundation of both diversification and concentration.

It is apparent that index-based investments, whether in ETFs that replicate markets or even in managed mutual funds that do little more than mirror the indexes with small adjustments to weights of BCE and Scotiabank, for example, are just reflections of the present. That is not a bad thing if you believe that energy stocks will rise again or that banks are properly valued. For the investor who wants to be relatively light on oil and to have a lot more electric power generation, the solutions are either to go to sector ETFs or to build a portfolio of appealing companies from scratch.

Deviating from market weights in an index takes a certain amount of courage. It is much like deciding to change the mix of goods for sale in your store. Some forward knowledge is needed, and that, like seeing through a fog, is easier said than done.

There is a powerful statistical rule and tool in finance. It's mean reversion, the concept that when a sector or a market and even a company is beaten down, it will eventually attract fresh investment and, in its business, find a way out of a hole and become respectable, even a market darling. The concept is quite valid, but it works best with mature markets and mature economies and with sectors that are economically viable. Mean reversion also works the other way. It predicts that overvalued stocks will tend to fall in market price.

All that is reason enough to be skeptical of making one big investment in any index or even in any asset class. Stocks have their days of sunshine, then unexpectedly crash, as they famously did in 1929, 1987, 1991, 1998,

2008, and, if we count a smaller flop, early 2016. The reasons change with the years and seasons. Point is, they happen. And when a crisis is severe enough, almost everything, even bonds, collapse as investors rush for the door out of every asset but cash and very short U.S. or Canada Treasury Bills with maturities of 30 days or less.

And that is why it is good to have money in assets that not only have survivability and growth, but also have the ability to pay dividends in times good and bad. The older you are, the less time there is for recovery. More utilities and banks perhaps, less cutting-edge no-dividend web stocks. But every crisis is different. Investors aware of the fragility of prosperity always spread their bets by use of mutual funds or ETFs or, if they have enough capital — say $100,000 at the least — a clutch of defensive assets like bonds or perhaps utility stocks whose returns are set and even guaranteed by regulators to provide some safety if — or when — yet another major crash happens.

> When a crisis is severe enough, almost everything, even bonds, collapse as investors rush for the door out of every asset but cash.

Initially, you can just add appropriate stocks to a portfolio based on broad-market, low-fee investment funds. They are already diversified. Later, with more experience, you may want to reduce broad-market funds and tailor your portfolio to your need for income, for income postponement to retirement, for deferral of capital gains, or even for acceleration of income or gains.

There is a risk in excess diversification. One is the problem of managing your brood. The other is the diminishing value of adding ever more stocks. Studies show that after a couple of dozen diversified stocks, you should have enough assets spread out to avoid overconcentration. Beyond that, every additional stock you buy tends to cut the advantage gained. The reasons are that one chartered bank is pretty much like another, one steel maker like another. One gold miner reflects the fate of others. There are important variations, and one famous market player, Peter Lynch of Fidelity Funds, famously said that if you like a company, buy three of the same, for if you pick just one, it will be the wrong one. But do not pile up similar companies, for diversification to the point of losing focus is no gain. Rather like the hardware store that moves into selling fabrics and running shoes, diversification can cause loss of focus. And even this rule has an exception, for at the time of writing Canadian Tire does all of this through its stores and those of clothing and related companies it owns. No law exists that cannot be broken.

TRENDS AND FASHIONS

Experienced investors try to put money into companies that offer desired combinations of growth and dividends, experienced management, leading-edge products, foreign-markets exposure, or other virtues. Some companies are trend participants and provide exposure to new small things that may become big things. Think of it as getting into railroads in 1880 or airlines in 1930. Good concepts, but the trends ended with superhighways built and maintained by taxpayers. Virtually free roads and low gas prices made truck shipments cheaper than train freight for many decades. Airline stocks went through decades of insolvencies. Some airlines fail because they can't pay their bills. Our own Canadian Airlines shut down in 2001 after pledging virtually every asset it had, right down to pictures on the walls, to creditors. Swissair flopped in 2002 and became Swiss. The Pan Am Lockerbie tragedy in 1988 — a bomber destroyed the plane — led passengers to quit because of what became infamous security lapses, and Pan Am declared bankruptcy in January 1991. The trend may be your friend, but trends, true to their names, are not forever.

As an investor, there will be trends that you will disagree with. You might be a dividend investor who shies away from resource stocks. By all means, do stand by your convictions and stick to what you know. However, it is unwise to argue with the market and try to profit from a trend reversal. Trends do reverse, but no trend has a clock running to time it. The trend will win in the short term. As John Maynard Keynes has said: "The market can stay irrational longer than you can stay solvent." Ignore this truism at your own peril.

The investor has to sort out what is trend and what is true. That is easier said than done. For example, an investor, especially one unsure of his or her own skills or thoughts about the market or a certain stock, may seek evidence to support a particular view. It happens on the way down, too. This seeking of support has been called confirmation bias. It arises when the investor has a conclusion and then shops for evidence that the conclusion is right. Confirmation bias is observable in the tendency of investors to stick with losers they love or to buy hot stocks others love. Intellectual honesty compels an investor to make his or her own decisions apart from the mass of other investors.

Another dimension of confirmation bias, and often its result, is the bandwagon effect. You can see it when many who are not aboard a trend rush to get on. This is late-stage investing, for the probability of a trend becoming a fixed force in the market tends to diminish over time. There

> Trends do reverse, but no trend has a clock running to time it — the trend will win in the short term.

are exceptions, of course. Early computer investment in the 1970s and 1980s was no fad, even though the players changed from Commodore and Atari to Google, now Alphabet Inc., and Facebook. Mean reversion usually clobbers the bandwagon effect, which, when in force, turns value stocks into growth stocks and growth stocks into mob momentum stocks with ever-rising valuations.

The toughest part of investing is discerning what is objectively true and what is your opinion of what is true. The process of unravelling perception from conclusion is the stuff of philosophy and psychology. Libraries of books have been written and careers built on this process of intellectual distillation. For any asset manager, the problem of perceiving what is true within observation comes down to profit and loss.

The sustainability of trends in general can be seen with a little bit of math. You can think of a rising stock or sector price as the upleg of a parabola. There are other geometries that work, but the parabola (a little up, then a rounded top, then down) works well enough. Put a flat line on the upleg and you have the tangent, or the rate of change, if you like. When the flat line or tangent goes horizontal, the parabola is headed down. You want to get off before the line is very negative. This is the concept, but wobbly stocks can have many uplegs and just as many downlegs. Using this little trick on annual stock prices is better, and better still is to use it on quarterly or annual sales over a period of several years. It is essential to get beyond statistical noise to make sound judgments.

No stock price rises forever, else a single share of the company would become worth more than the rest of the world. The end of the Japanese property stock market boom in 1989 was inevitable after a 224 percent increase since 1985, a rise heavily dependent on inflated Japanese metropolitan real estate prices. If you plot out prices of shares that seem to defy gravity, it is time to sell or, even more certainly, not to buy into the trend. It is more likely to be the end of the boom than any midpoint.

Investors who buy stocks with no dividends are betting on price changes and nothing but. Whether they are long and waiting for a price move up or short and hoping for a price decline, they are making bets as risky as those in blackjack, where the turn of a card makes a winner or a loser, or roulette, where a ball tumbling around a circle and then falling into a slot determines the outcome.

THE VALUE OF DIVIDENDS

Dividends mitigate losses and add to gains. Early stage companies often have no distributable income, and many mature companies, famously Warren Buffett's Berkshire Hathaway Inc., prefer to reinvest than to distribute income. One can create a kind of periodic payment like a dividend by writing — that is, selling — covered calls. They are the right to take a stock away from its owner, paid for by a call premium. Options investing is a skill set of its own, but it is sufficient to say that call premiums are paid by investors, not the companies themselves, and are the antithesis of buy and hold. The investor who takes a small premium for writing a covered call gives up the right to own the stock as long as he or she likes. If and when the stock hits the target price, the call writer, that is, the person who sold the right to take the stock, gives up ownership and dividend. The stock can be repurchased, of course, but the process only adds complexity to what would be a buy-and-hold strategy.

The dividend in cash (not as a percentage) divided by stock price is the yield. The range of yields goes from miniscule for early stage growing companies and those that hoard cash for reinvestment to others that have customary handsome dividends like BCE Inc. — about 5 percent — to stocks with falling prices whose dividends divided by declining stock price are both tantalizing and a sign that investors believe the good times won't last. As a general rule, if a stock yield climbs above 6 percent, investors who observe relatively low stock prices believe there is trouble ahead. At 8 percent or 10 percent, there is serious trouble and the dividend is very likely to be cut or cancelled. Lofty dividends indicate the denominator, the stock price, has fallen a great deal. The dividend expressed as percentage yield has become a warning sign.

> As a general rule, if a stock yield climbs above 6 percent, investors who observe relatively low stock prices believe there is trouble ahead.

You can think of dividend investing as a life stage process. You can accept stocks with low or zero dividends early in life and then migrate to hefty dividend payers in retirement. Some dividend-paying stocks such as electrical utilities and telecommunications providers tend to have hefty dividend yields in the 3.5 percent to 5 percent range by tradition. There is a note of caution, however, for telcos and power companies tend to have heavy long-term debt. When making any investment in a heavily indebted company, investigate the debt metrics, especially how much in loans or bonds are due and when they are due. There are no hard and fast rules on debt metrics, but it is certain that a company that has to devote a vast share of operating income to debt service or a company that is buying shares back to boost the stock price and dividend returns at the expense of adding heavily to debt is one to be avoided. A debt-to-equity ratio of 1 to 1 is fairly neutral. If it rises to 2 to 1 or 3 to 1 or more and if debt service costs are a large part of operating earnings, beware. A downturn means that debt service costs can prevent or reduce dividend payouts.

We need a note of caution at this point, for there are situations in which dividends are disadvantageous. For example, a fully taxable account held by a person who receives Old Age Security, which is income tested, starts to be eroded by the OAS clawback and disappears when income reaches about $122,000. Dividends are grossed up on the first page of the Canadian individual income tax return by 38 percent and thus accelerate the erosion of OAS. For such investors, postponement of stock returns by avoidance of high dividend stocks is sensible. Taking prospective capital gains at any time in future makes more sense.

Not all stocks are equal in how they are watched by the community of investors. It follows that very widely watched companies such as chartered banks and the big telcos have few secrets. Public scrutiny by managers of investment funds, university endowments, and pension plans all help to keep corporate management honest. There is much less scrutiny of non-regulated companies and even less for small caps and companies making ephemeral products such as handbags and fashion accessories. Economies do not live or die if a fashion house flares up or fails.

CRITICAL RATIOS

The toughest part of stock analysis is deciding which company in an industry to buy when its price or prospects are attractive and which to sell when you need cash or if its price has gone to what you think are unsustainable levels. Quantitative investors use multiple screens to locate companies whose shares have many characteristics such as low price to earnings or low price to sales. There are many screens for making trading decisions, including the best known, price to earnings, but also price to cash flow, price to sales, and return on sales. There are many more, but we need to focus on a few to show what works and what tends not to work well. We want to avoid complexity, which can be a bar to understanding. Simplicity is a virtue in the jungle of numbers produced by capital markets.

There are many ways to value stocks, but the most used is earnings per share. If it rises, investors tend to bid up the share price. If earnings go down, odds are very strong that share price will follow. Earnings forecasts by analysts who are supposed to know their business are at best "interpretive," to use a kind word, and at worst dead wrong. We show their records later in this chapter.

Earnings forecasts have themselves become an indicator along with price momentum. Thus, stocks can soar if their quarterly or annual reports beat estimates as investors pile in, which tends to make the price rise further. If earnings reports are lower than estimates, the herd flees. What the mob is doing is reflected in price momentum. Positive price momentum tends to push up both share price and the p/e multiple. That's a handsome reward, for higher multiples are a double whammy — higher earnings plus higher multiple of "p" to "e" means a bigger reward. At least until the trend reverses, when it turns downright perverse and market cannibals begin to short stocks by borrowing shares, selling them now and hoping to buy shares cheaper in future to pay back the loans.

Price to earnings, for all its flaws, is nevertheless the most widely used of stock value measures. It is a guide, but one filled with peril, rather like a compass that is right some of the time and wrong the rest. The idea is that if share price divided by earnings per share is too high, you will overpay for shares, and if the ratio is too low, investors think there is something very wrong.

Historically, p/e's could be interpreted as follows: below, say, a p/e of 10, if you buy shares, you are disagreeing with other investors who have sold off the stock. If you pay 10 to 20, you are in with the mass of conservative investors. If you pay 30, 40, 50, or more times earnings, you agree with other investors that a stock is really worth having. And at a p/e of hundreds, as Amazon.com and Netflix are today, you are prepared to wait for earnings to rise sufficiently to bring the ratios down to livable levels. Very high p/e ratios indicate that investors are willing to pay for a Niagara of earnings to come. The higher the ratio, the more the risk, for earnings may be disappointing or may never appear. Recall the dot-coms when investors paid fortunes for stocks with no "e" at all. In the end, raw earnings, with all the manipulation possible, is a start on valuation but not the end of the story.

Note that companies can take shares out of the market by buybacks. This is popular with investors for it means that there are fewer mouths to feed, so the earnings per share will tend to rise. The implication, of course, is that the company is admitting that it can't match the return investors might get in other investments. Return of capital can also be a happy event, though, a sort of present to shareholders. But beware companies that pay for buybacks by borrowing and adding debt. Nothing is a free ride.

Earnings can also indicate payback time. If you pay 5 times earnings, then excluding dividends, you are saying that the company will earn back its price in five years. If p/e is 10, you have to wait ten years. At a p/e of 200, it's two centuries if earnings don't rise. And even if the 100 p/e stock does have great years — say earnings doubling in a few years — you may then have to wait only fifty years to get your money back. Some company earnings do justify these multiples. They tend to be techs, but none of the very high p/e stocks can have significant dividend yields. These are gambles.

> In the end, raw earnings, with all the manipulation possible, is a start on valuation but not the end of the story.

The problem with p/e is that the earnings part is too easily manipulated by companies. They can accelerate sales by cutting profit margins or even by done-deal "sales" where there has been no delivery and no payment. That's fraudulent, but it happens. Companies can delay recognition of costs, capitalize some costs onto their balance sheets, and do other tricks to manipulate earnings.[4] In an effort to make earnings worth more as a predictive device, analysts have come up with several distillations of the concept, including EBITDA, short for earnings before interest, taxes, depreciation of plant and equipment, and amortization. EBITDA is not published by companies in their accounts for it is not a GAAP (generally accepted accounting principles) measure. However, EBITDA and its offspring can be found in research reports from stock brokerages. It is easily found for most companies.

EBITDA gets closer to showing true profitability of core operations, as opposed to earnings juiced up by accountants, because it eliminates the effect of various kinds of interest payments, tax juggling in different jurisdictions, asset write-downs as depreciation, and costs shifts due to goodwill charges involved in takeovers. If EBITDA is negative, that is a bad sign, but if it is positive, it means not much more than that the company is paying its bills. By minimizing capital costs, it can overstate earnings. There are also variations on EBITDA that take out the depreciation or amortization and others that insert measures of restructuring costs. The question for the right measure to use for earnings is a crusade for an elusive grail.

Given the inadequacy of all the variations of earnings, many investors and analysts prefer to look at price to cash flow. Cash flow is harder for accountants to fiddle and, more importantly, it measures actual money coming into the company. If cash flow is strong, then dividends may be sustainable even if earnings slump.

Other measures are price to book value, which is a balance sheet measure. It means a good deal for comparing banks, but it's not too valuable for comparing software companies that are just desks, computers, and the unmeasurable worth of what is inside of the brains of their employees. And it's even less valuable if the company pays its "workers" via contracts rather than payrolls.

For that, and just for statistical reasons, price to sales (p/s) turns out to be a more reliable indicator of value and future returns than p/e or even price to cash flow, which is less manipulatable than price to earnings. In a pathbreaking study of investing by p/e, p/cf, and p/s, the distinguished American money manager James P. O'Shaughnessy, author of *What Works on Wall Street*, demonstrated that price to sales, a measure of how much business you are buying for your investment, works best.[5] In a test of several value rankings, including price to earnings, price to book value, and price to cash flow, O'Shaughnessy came up with the valuable conclusion that buying stocks with the lowest price-to-sales ratios produced better returns than use of the other valuations.

In contrast, buying stocks with the highest price-to-sales ratios produced results that were, in O'Shaughnessy's words, "toxic." In one test period from December 31, 1980, through December 31, 1984, $10,000 invested in a data set, the S&P Compustat All-Stocks Universe with the highest p/s ratios, fell 70 percent even as the Universe itself grew by more than 50 percent. The results of buying low p/s stocks versus high p/s stocks are variable by period, but there is a rule of thumb: Most stocks will have p/s ratios below 2. If you are conservative, you will not pay more than 3 times sales per share.[6] The concept of using price to sales rather than more distilled metrics — remember, profit and cash flow are a fraction of sales, assuming a company is efficient and generates a return to its investors — is just one metric. There are others. Each is a filter. For each investor, the filters may be different. That means one should develop a set of rules or guidelines for investing.

Here is a set of rules designed to hold down risks:

> Other investors want to be in new industries where capital is fresh and products new. Those industries are on the internet.

- Stocks must have price to sales below 2 and 6 at the very most, and price to earnings below 30.
- Industries must be growing, with useful, understandable products.
- Stocks must not defy understanding.
- Portfolios should not be overloaded with favoured industries, such as financial services.
- Stocks must have dividends sufficient to provide a yield of 1.5 percent, and preferably twice or thrice that, with no adverse economic trends in view to cause dividend cuts.
- Regulators must not be trying to kill the company or its products — that lets tobacco companies out.
- Profit margins must be sustainable — that lets out airlines that soar or fall inversely to the trend of fuel prices.
- Finally, the companies must be price makers, able to set the prices of what they sell, rather than price receivers, as almost all commodity companies are.

Other investors want to be in new industries where capital is fresh and products new. Those industries are on the internet — look at the successes of Alphabet (formerly Google), Facebook, and Netflix. But other tech ideas have come and gone. Remember Blockbuster? Renting videos flopped when internet-based rentals replaced store visits. They became the buggy whips of entertainment.

TIME AND MEASURES OF VALUE

Price to earnings and price to sales are relatively current valuations. Some investors prefer to look at price to book value, alias price to book. The p/b ratio is just market price of a share divided by the book value of equity per share at a given moment. On the positive side, price to book is a fairly standard measure, while price to earnings has many variants. So the standardization of p/b is recognized everywhere.

Price to book is not a current valuation. It is based on ledgered historical cost. There is a problem of updating costs. The book value of equity is the original proceeds received by the company when it issued stock plus earnings made since then and reduced by dividend paid out during the period. Stock buybacks reduce the book value of equity, large losses deducted from the company's value reduce book value, and shares of other firms and unrealized gains or losses of marketable securities also increase or decrease book value. If a firm chooses to accelerate depreciation, that will reduce book value. Likewise, slowing depreciation will raise book value from what it might otherwise be and thus raise the value of a firm's assets.[7] Low price to book value is a good screen, but it is most appropriate for examining firms with heavy investments in fixed and relatively solid assets. On that basis, it can generate excess returns over broad indices. For firms in service industries or generating profits with human capital that cannot be depreciated in any accounting sense, it is not appropriate. The greatest criticism of price to book is that it sets a ratio on what is ultimately the liquidation value of a company. Fundamental valuation it is, but we think it is not a leading valuation, but part of a filter for value. Low price to book, in the end, is worth knowing. If a firm's p/b is below 1, as it is in many capital-intensive utility industries, that is a sign of relative value. If it is high, as it is in drug and medical services companies where ratios of 2 to 5 are common, it is only one part of valuation.

TAKING OVER YOUR PORTFOLIO

Our chapter on stocks and indeed the entire content of *Cherished Fortune* is aimed at helping the investor take over an investment portfolio. In a sense, it is like moving from letting others run your store to taking over management and doing so with the knowledge of what you need and how to get to your own goals.

The problems of self-management are partly the technical problems of finding stocks that have the right characteristics and partly the psychological problem of keeping your own vision and goals in focus. There are innumerable tip sheets, especially among small cap stock promoters; theories hyped by stock-picking letters; notions of swift gains wrapped in books you have to buy; and touts who are paid to steer web traffic to dubious investments. How do you remain true to yourself?

> The problems of self-management are partly the technical problems of finding stocks with the right characteristics and partly the psychological problem of keeping your vision and goals in focus.

The first rule of running a portfolio is to create circuit breakers; that is, rules you never violate. For example:

1. Never put more than 10 percent of your portfolio into any one company. If you do, your risk rises.
2. Never put more than 30 percent of your portfolio into any one sector. This, too, raises your risk.
3. Review your portfolio every three months or six months, or even once a year.
4. Decide if you will let winners ride or sell those with the biggest gains and buy more of stocks that have dropped the most. Every decision has to be reviewed on the facts.
5. Selling some or all of your winners at least to get your initial money back is simple price arbitrage and it works.
6. Monitor laggards. You can reset the rule to sell half of your winners, keep half, and buy just half as much again as you hold of the losers. This way, you always stay in the game.
7. Limit risk by keeping your portfolio relatively low priced or at least at a lower cost base than if you let winners ride. Nothing, after all, is forever.
8. If you want to buy a stock, know what the company does.

Make sure it will last. In running a portfolio, as in running a store, you will come across fashion trends, such as those in asset classes. That was what pumped up dot-coms from 1998 to 2000, no matter that some companies had no profits, others no sales, and still others no business plans. It was crazy then and is crazy now. Brokerage houses, financial publications, folks you may know, and outright hucksters will tell you that new web retailers or some new chain of restaurants specializing in vegetarian cuisine or a new style of barbeque sweeping all of Texas is the thing to be in. There is every reason to check out the stories by reading relevant publications and checking the financial press and the companies' own websites to see what's up.

9. Set a measuring stick and stay with it. Stay with a valuation rule. There are scores of theories on how to buy stocks, from bedrock-solid concepts of seeking value stocks with low ratios of price to earnings to looking for hot stocks in play. They all work, but they do not work all the time. The best theories are the ones you understand. Of all of those, price to sales works best.[8] Why? Because earnings can be manipulated by accountants who defer costs and accelerate sales. Cash flow is better but has the same vulnerabilities. Sales, on the other hand, are top-line data, and any acceleration can usually be spotted by comparing receivables with sales. If receivables are rising faster than sales, something is wrong. Perhaps customers are not paying. Perhaps there are reasons for delaying payments. Remember: you don't have to be right. You just have to avoid being wrong!

10. Set rules for identifying promising stocks. They may include the following:

   a. Companies must have a record of rising sales and profits for ten years.

   b. Companies should have a moat around their businesses; that is, an unassailable position as maker or doer of something.

   c. Management should be experienced. Check the annual

reports. See who is running the business into which you want to put your money. Look at the list of directors and what company is the auditor. If the directors are not credible or the auditors are an outfit you've never heard of, stay away. All of this is in the annual report of each company.

d. Dividends should be rising and a reasonable fraction of earnings. When dividends take more than 80 percent of earnings, beware. The dividends may not be sustainable if earnings drop.

e. The company is operating in the present with products and services people want to buy. This is just common sense.

11. Set guidelines for companies you may want to drop:

a. Collapsing sales or profits: Find out why. If the reasons are long term — for example, the company's products are out of date — the fundamental reason to own the business is gone. Sell.

b. Major criminal or civil prosecutions: This is self-evident. If the top brass is going to jail — think of scandals like Enron, a largely fictitious energy trader once lauded by the business press — you should be gone. Try to beat the cops. Leave at the first hint of scandal.

c. Major new competition: Old-line retailers are being eaten by Amazon.com. Take your money and run.

d. Low commodity price: If the price of the commodity the company deals in seems too low for the cost structure of the company and there is no fix in sight, sell.

e. Accounting manipulation: The stock's price is rising not because of solid market conditions for what it sells or does but because management is juicing up the stock price by stock buybacks. Taking 10 percent of the stock off the market means that the remaining 90 percent of shares' will have a comparable boost in earnings.

f. Nobody wants the stuff: If it is rooted in the past, stay away or get out fast.

FALSE RECALL AND HOW TO AVOID IT

Some investors remember their wins, while others cannot forget their losses. The danger in this form of myopia is the lack of balance of one's judgment and, worse, the inability or compromised ability to learn from mistakes and to avoid giving excess weight to one's successes. The lesson of a long shot on a hot stock or dubious bond that produces a hefty profit is that it may encourage you to stick with long shots and the high risks they bear. Chance has to be balanced with wisdom. If investment markets were easily predictable, asset prices would be close to ideal or perfect and all commitments of money would be wasted. Just as the storekeeper has to keep studying the market and the costs of running the business, the investor needs to see his or her own commitments as both luck and intelligent selection.

> When investors cannot forget their losses, the danger in this form of myopia is the inability to learn from mistakes.

That nothing is forever demonstrates the point. The top stocks of the 1960s, the Nifty Fifty, became drudges by 1990. Winners that get admitted to the S&P 500 after a good year ironically then have bad years, while losers kicked out of the S&P 500 then have good years.

Market forecasters' own records are problematic. A Goldman Sachs guru, Abby Joseph Cohen, dubbed the "Chief Jester of the Internet Bubble" before the dot-coms popped in 2000, later called for stocks to rise strongly in 2008. Elaine Garzarelli, the only prominent analyst on Wall Street to predict the crash of 1987, later produced nothing worth mentioning. Garzarelli was fired by her employer, Shearson Lehman Brothers Inc. in 1994. Fourteen years later, Lehman Brothers itself collapsed.

THE BALANCE OF TRUST

The famous New York Yankees baseball icon Yogi Berra is given credit for having said "making predictions is very hard, especially about the future." The record of analysts is not encouraging. Most of the time, they recommend buying or holding companies they follow, often because their employers do the investment banking for the same firms. It does not help their employers to try to sell shares their analysts disparage.

Not surprisingly, research on the accuracy of stock price forecasting shows it to be a swamp of dismal outcomes. A major stock research house, the Franklin, Massachusetts–based CXO Advisory Group, found the following:[9]

- Across all forecasts, accuracy was worse than the proverbial flip of a coin — just under 47 percent.
- The average guru also had a forecasting accuracy of about 47 percent.
- The distribution of forecasting accuracy by the gurus looks very much like what you would expect from random outcomes. That makes it very difficult to tell if there is any skill present.
- The highest accuracy score was 68 percent and the lowest was 22 percent.
- There were many well-known forecasters in the sample:
- James Dines, founder of *The Dines Letter*. According to his website, "He is truly a living legend ... one of the most-accurate and highly regarded Security Investment Analysts today." His forecasting accuracy score was 50 percent. Not quite the stuff of which legends are made.
- Ben Zacks, a co-founder of well-known Zacks Investment Research and senior strategist and portfolio manager at Zacks Wealth Management Group. His score was 50 percent.
- Bob Brinker, host of the widely syndicated *MoneyTalk* radio program and editor of the *Marketimer* newsletter. His score was 53 percent.
- Jeremy Grantham, chairman of GMO LLC, a global investment management firm. His score was 44 percent.
- Dr. Mark Faber, publisher of the *Gloom, Boom and Doom Report*. His score was 47 percent.
- Jim Cramer, CNBC superstar. His score was 47 percent.
- John Mauldin, well-known author. His score was just 40 percent.

- Gary Shilling, *Forbes* columnist. His score was 37 percent.
- Abby Joseph Cohen, partner and chief U.S. investment strategist at Goldman Sachs. Her score was 35 percent.
- Robert Prechter, publisher of the *Elliott Wave Theorist*. He brought up the rear with a score of 21 percent.

Only five of the sixty-eight gurus had scores above 60 percent (among them was a serious scholar, David Dreman, with a score of 64 percent), yet twelve had scores below 40 percent.

> The record of analysts is not encouraging — most of the time, they recommend buying or holding companies they follow.

The takeaway on all this is that fresh thinking may be as valid as old thoughts. It's your store, after all. Run it your way. Confine your work to building a portfolio with defined parameters; for example, solid dividends backing up price growth expectations, time spans of at least one stock market cycle of thirty-six to forty-eight months or even up to sixty months, ample liquidity elsewhere so you will not be forced to sell, and suitable tax planning to avoid having to raise cash to meet unexpected bills from the government. Then you are on the way to building a stock portfolio that is poised to rise, has known risks, and furnishes sufficient diversification through numbers of stocks held or through managed mutual funds or index ETFs, so that a particular company flop or market downturn will not do too much damage to your plans and needs.

The time to develop this portfolio will have to match your growing experience and needs. Don't expect that you can do it in a week or even a month. Work out a plan, buy an asset, see how it fares, then buy the next. Spreading buys over time is a form of diversification, price averaging by a common name.

Your target return with this kind of buying in and buying conservatively should approximate the long-run return of equity investing. That is 2 percent to 3 percent for dividends and 5 percent to 7 percent for stock prices, each before inflation. Add them up to 7 percent to 10 percent and take off the inflation, and you can expect a 7 percent return over the long run. That means capital can double in a decade. You can use other assets such as real estate to seek higher returns at the cost of complexity, managing tenants, and illiquidity, or government bonds with a lower return but the guarantee of reversion to cash at maturity; that is, a kind of automatic sale. Each asset class has its characteristics, but stocks, in spite of their tapestry of accounting and management, are indispensable for enlarging one's wealth over time.

With so many losers among the forecasters, one can either spend time seeking the promised prophet or, as we have suggested, do the basic legwork independently. If nothing else, this homework will help you understand what mutual fund managers do and how ETFs both improve on and sometimes fail to improve on the records of management.

CHAPTER 6

Real Estate: Huge Rewards and Lots of Headaches — How Fortunes Are Made and Lost

Real estate appeals to the instinct to have something solid rather than the theories of corporate ownership in stocks or promises to pay on which bonds are built. You buy acreage to rent to farmers or a building with apartments that can be rented. A condo may seem priced advantageously in terms of the rent it can generate. You can buy a strip mall with medical offices or, going a little further into collective ownership, you can buy into real estate trusts and companies that own office buildings. The core concept is that land is scarce; that, as the saying goes, they're not making it anymore. The shareholder's only right is to vote for directors. But when you own a building or a condo, a tract of land or even a right to buy or to develop land, you have something tangible. You can touch it and live in a dwelling if you can't rent it. None of that works for stocks or bonds.

THE IDEA OF OWNERSHIP

The philosophy of investing in land, which is that it is fixed in amount, is not right. We have to say this right up front. Global warming is eroding and even submerging land in Florida while exposing new land as the Arctic Ocean opens to navigation. In some cities, rentable space grows upward with skyscrapers as air rights take over from land rights.

Owning land or buildings has been the basis of great fortunes in much of the world since records began to be kept in Babylon a millennium and a half before the birth of Christ. As a group, with the exception of a New York tycoon who made a splash in reality television and American presidential politics, real estate moguls are quiet, unbelievably rich, and secure with diversified holdings mostly in office properties but also shopping centres and even hospital land and buildings. The only other industries that have produced so many great fortunes are high tech and casino ownership — which is not gambling at all; it's usually a sure thing for the owners.

The mechanics of real estate investing are straightforward. You find land or buildings for sale, work out the flow of income from rents, work out costs, then borrow as much money as is prudent from the viewpoints of your accountant and your bank or other lenders, and sit back to count the money rolling in. That is the concept, but it does not always work out that way.

It has to be said that because real estate is tangible property, there is liability for injuries that may happen on property or in a building one owns, there can be pollution or other environmental issues, and there can be exposure to fires and other mayhem. If you own physical property, you need to buy insurance. That's one cost that investments in pure financial assets do not carry.

Owning something stuck to the ground, or the ground itself, has special risks. Consider the egregious case of Love Canal, not far from Niagara Falls, which was found to have toxic levels of benzene and other chemicals in its soil and ground water. The neighbourhood had been used as a dump for numerous chemicals by a large American company. Heavy snowmelt in 1977 brought toxic chemicals to the surface, widespread illness was found to have been caused by the contamination, and the neighbourhood was condemned and evacuated. Occupants were compensated by the first ever American Superfund created by then-president Jimmy Carter in 1978. Numerous carcinogenic compounds were found in the ground and in oozing black muck that leaked into neighbourhood basements. Eventually, the U.S. government relocated more than 800 families and paid them for the loss of their homes. All houses in the neighbourhood were demolished in the cleanup process. All this preceded the 1986 Chernobyl disaster.[1] The lesson: Oil refineries, chemical plants, slaughterhouses, and many heavy industrial factories do not make good neighbours. Local residential housing prices tend to reflect this fact.

Love Canal is probably as bad as adverse neighbourhood change can be. On the other side of the coin is gentrification; that is, the conversion of a crummy neighbourhood to something trendy, where the cognoscenti go and developers hasten to turn squatters' hovels into trendy and pricey homes. For those who stay through a period of decay, gentrification can create huge profits. Think Cabbagetown in Toronto, a now venerable example of what was once down-and-out housing that is now upscale. The process of urban upscaling has turned squalid streets chic in Toronto's Leslieville, too. It has not yet happened to Toronto's notorious neighbourhood around Jane and Finch, but in time it could. In Berlin, Prenzlauer Berg, formerly a dumpy part of East Germany, has become one of the trendiest neighbourhoods. For developers who move in early and take a stake, or potential homeowners who buy and hold to sell to upscale bidders or to build their own dwelling, gentrification can be profitable. Policies that restrict urban sprawl inevitably put a premium on existing neighbourhoods. Existing owners who are patient can have the pleasure of seeing modest homes sell for seven-figure sale prices. In Vancouver, that process is merely routine.

LEVERAGE

The tool of fortune is leverage — that is, borrowing from banks or other lenders, or, for large projects, selling shares in your real estate company or debt via bonds — but many investors get their estimates wrong and wind up bankrupt. Just ask Paul Reichmann, builder of First Canadian Place — the tallest building in Canada when completed in 1975. Reichmann's company, Olympia & York, then expanded to New York and Tokyo, becoming the biggest private office builder in the world.

In the 1990s, Olympia & York built the world's largest office complex, Canary Wharf in London, but a worldwide recession made it impossible to fill more than half the office space. They had used their wealth to buy oil company Gulf Canada Resources. In May 1992, Olympia & York filed for bankruptcy. The Canary Wharf project collapsed under $20 billion owed to creditors. The family's eminence grise, Paul Reichmann, lost most of his personal fortune. The lesson: Leverage is good, for it enables what amounts to a down payment or other owner equity to control much more capital through borrowing. Leverage is bad when the loan to value ratio is too high and income from the property in question becomes insufficient to pay costs, especially interest on loans. In short, an investor may be able to put off the plumber, but the major lenders with loans secured against property always get paid.

> Kicking the tires of real estate investments is essential to avoiding the fate of failed investors and what was in almost every case insufficient research.

With all of that said, real estate remains a very attractive concept. Depending on the use, the owner/developer can decide with which industry or industries the project will be in partnership. The investor can buy residential condos or even convert a basement to a rentable apartment using borrowed money for the job, invest in companies that lease office towers in Calgary, where energy prices and production influence occupancy rates, or buy into companies that lease office space in Toronto, where banks and insurance companies are big tenants.

Each component of the real estate business has distinctive financial determinants. We'll list them in order of importance by industry. Kicking the tires of each potential real estate investment is essential to avoiding the fate of failed investors and what was in almost every case insufficient research. As William Zeckendorf, a fabled New York developer, and his son, William Zeckendorf Jr., both of whom went bankrupt, observed, there is no amount of borrowed money that can save a project when the tides of business or eve of fundamental economics turn against it.[2]

Because real estate investing is built on borrowed money, perhaps more than in any other sector of the economy, interest rates are the fundamental determinant of financial life. Low interest rates make loans cheap, big projects do-able, small condos affordable — witness the Toronto real estate boom and the mid-six-figure prices of units with 500 or 600 square feet of living space — and risks too easy to take.

INTEREST RATE TRENDS

Long-term interest rates remain near historically low levels, the result of central bank moves to rescue the world's banking system after the 2008–2009 global meltdown driven by rotten mortgages issued to people who could not pay them. Low interest rates drive investors to put their money into equity — stocks, real estate, and other uses. Moreover, a widespread focus, even a mania, for saving for retirement aided by RRSPs in Canada, IRAs in the U.S., and comparable products in other countries has increased the supply of loanable funds. There is a great deal of cash sloshing around in the world and it is cheap to hire. Banks happily lend for homes and business projects, but when interest rates rise to their historic levels, several percent higher than now, and ten-year Government of Canada and U.S. Treasury bonds return to their historic range of 4 percent to 5 percent, banks will demand more interest, and overleveraged and inefficiently run projects will fail.

What's more, when a lot of investors want to get out of their real estate holdings, they will come up against the single most distinctive characteristic of property: it is illiquid. You can sell one hundred shares of a bank in an instant and a bond in perhaps a couple of instants, depending on the bond. To sell real estate can take weeks or more of pricing, bargaining, negotiating, closing … et cetera. The recent pattern of sales in Vancouver and Toronto, where houses have been sold in the same day they have gone up for sale, is atypical.

There are shortcuts to liquidity. For example, if you have partners in a deal, you and they may be able to agree to first refusal buyouts. If they stand ready to buy you out or you them, the liquidity problem can be patched over. Unless everybody in the partnership is short of cash and credit.

The alternative to sale is to add a second mortgage to the property. Typically, that involves credit checks, a willing lender, and payment of what can be 10 percent to 15 percent from a specialty lender. The second mortgage lender's interest is subordinate to that of the first lender, so there is more risk. The borrower is seen as stressed in some way, otherwise they would not have to seek the second mortgage. If you have to pay 10 percent or even more, sale may be the better route.

COST CONTROLS AND PRICING

It has been said that "a thing is worth what someone will pay for it." The blandness and obviousness of the statement conceals the inner truth that every investment asset has to be paid for. When investors buy a building with a mortgage, for example, a $10 million small professional office building, with 25 percent upfront for the down payment and 75 percent borrowed at prime (recently 3.5 percent plus 2 percent, net 5.5 percent), they set the cost floor for subsequent rents. Lenders do stress tests to judge stability of cash flow, but there are times, typically in massive recessions when all asset classes tumble, that even conservatively financed real estate projects can't make their mortgage payments.

There is a security blanket for real estate speculation or investment, as you prefer, and that is cost control. High leverage — for example, borrowing 80 percent of a project's cost — creates more risk than borrowing just 50 percent. That leverage is distinct and focused for real estate projects and unfocused but just as powerful for the economy as a whole. As stocks rise during a boom, the various metrics like price to earnings, price to sales, and price to cash flow all rise together. The higher the multiples rise, the deeper stock prices will tumble.

At the time this sentence was written, the widely used Case Shiller cyclically adjusted price earnings ratio, the CAPE index, is at 30, almost twice the historic average of 17 since 1881. In this environment, assets acquired with borrowed money appear expensive. To build a margin of safety, investors need to pay less to buy into an asset, or they can borrow less. In this game, loan to value (LTV) can make or break a project.

Another way to look at a residential real estate investment is the relationship of property price to rent. As *The Economist* noted, that relationship in Canada is at its highest level since 2008 and is higher than in similar markets in the U.S., Australia, and Britain.[3] What is driving up the ratio is not rising interest rates; rather, it is the prices owners are paying to earn rents. The ratio, however, is not a pure expression of the market, for rent controls in Toronto and other large cities suppress rents. Still, the principle exists for Canada as a whole. The cost of earning rent has soared just as interest rates have fallen. Low mortgage interest costs should facilitate purchases of houses and condos, but prices have risen faster than interest rates have dropped. For renters who would be owners, it is a perverse cycle.

> There is a security blanket for real estate speculation or investment, as you prefer, and that is cost control.

The process of finding and pricing a rental property is complex and requires both a sharp pencil and a sense of what is happening in the city, town, village, or, for that matter, countryside; zoning rules now and as they may change; desirability of the location; prices of competing properties; rent trends; economic influences on the housing market; and trends in local desirability (that is, neighbourhood change).

Every variable but one may be favourable, but that one variable can wreck an investment. Take the case of Detroit. Crime turned a once proud city into a vast real estate bargain basement. But the problem remains — who would risk life and fortune on a city abandoned by much business and most lenders?[4]

PROPERTY MARKET MECHANICS

Real estate markets are local. Even huge real estate companies with dozens of shopping centres, office buildings, and rental apartments are webs of local investment. A rental unit in Toronto with its broadly based economy is not the same in terms of price trends, price sustainability, taxation, jobs for tenants, and weather exposure as the same unit in Edmonton or Vancouver. Just after the nadir of the American mortgage meltdown crisis, thousands of investors descended on former housing hotspots to snatch up repossessed houses in Arizona, Nevada, and California. Those who decided to use them as vacation homes got good deals.

> Running a rental is not a seat-of-the-pants business: to get it right — and to avoid loss — records are essential.

Scale is the difference between owing a rental unit down the block and clearing the snow yourself for a tenant and owning two hundred rental units and having to use contractors for every maintenance job that comes along. The larger the unit or units and the more numerous they are, the stricter the accounting needed not only for your own business management, but also for tax collectors, insurance underwriters, and repair contractors.

For software programs to help manage a property, see buildium.com, managerplus.com, or capterra.com. This is just a sample of what is available. Running a rental is not a seat-of-the-pants business. To get it right — and to avoid loss and get your taxes right — records are essential.

BORROWING

Leverage is key to the profitability of real estate investments. Down payments for commercial and rental property are generally higher than for owner-occupied residential property. The reasons are philosophical in part, for banks and other lenders assume that the owner of a house or condo will be reluctant to walk away from their home. Moreover, homes tend to be owned by individuals rather than by corporations. In Canada, lenders can seize property and sue for any deficiency of the loan. In the United States, generally, lenders must choose to seize or sue homeowners deficient in payments owed on their homes. It is a great difference.

How much to borrow for an investment is more than a banking rule. A borrower who takes the maximum leverage confronts the lender with a different problem than the borrower who has very little left on a loan. In the first case, if a house has a $500,000 estimated market price and a loan for $400,000 outstanding, the lender is taking a risk that it can get at least $400,000 for the home. If there is only, say, $50,000 left on a defaulted loan, the lender can get what amounts to a coverage of ten times the outstanding amount if it has to liquidate the loan. In fairness and in law, the lender would then have to pay the debtor what is left after settlement of the debt and costs.

Leverage poses a risk to both parties in a transaction, but it also gives the borrower a lot of power. In our $500,000 house, which we will assume is bought for rental, if rent is $30,000 a year, the owner has paid 100 percent of the house price, $500,000, and the return per year after all costs including interest on the loan is $15,000, the return on the owner's equity will be $15,000 divided by $500,000, or 3 percent. If the owner has borrowed 50 percent, then the return after all costs will be 6 percent. In the first case, the owner is just covering inflation at 3 percent even before any thoughts of income tax. In the second, inflation is covered and there should be some margin of profit even after tax.

Many real estate investors are willing to run zero profit or even slightly negative cash flow operations in the expectation that their properties will appreciate. In some markets, such as Toronto and Vancouver, dramatic price gains have covered costs and many management sins, poor accounting, tenant damage, loss of rent due to vacancy, and more. The investor who conceives of rental income as subsidy for anticipated capital gains is in fact a gambler on real estate price trends. And while it is true that, over periods of many decades, most property prices rise, there are times when interest rates spike and force property price cuts, and when governments impose rent controls that restrict what landlords can charge or add transaction costs when properties are sold to cut down on price gains achieved through property flipping.

Figuring out what a property is worth is often laborious. Unlike stocks, which are priced and published on boards and websites every second of the trading day; options, which are both published and easily computed; and even bonds, which have published prices for large government and corporate issues; real estate pricing is both science and art. In any given locale, it is usually only a tiny fraction of all properties that change hands every day or week or month. So published real estate prices are samples rather than exact dollars at which one can trade. Moreover, because no two formerly occupied — that is, used — properties are identical, every price one finds has to be adjusted for the condition and desirability of the property in question.

There are other differences in comparing investments in real estate with investments in stocks and bonds. Stocks or exchange traded funds allow you to invest just a few hundred dollars or even less in mutual funds. You can mix and match and have foreign stocks and domestic bonds with a mouse click if you use a computer to trade.

In real estate, the chunks of money involved are large. Leverage adds to returns and to risk. Going in and out of property usually involves lawyers and their fees, plus an accountant to review books for commercial deals and those fees. There may be appraisals. There are property transaction costs, title searches in some jurisdictions, building inspection costs, and perhaps repair costs to cover. The front-end costs for investing in real estate far outstrip what it takes to make a sensible purchase of shares in a stock or some units of a mutual fund or exchange traded fund.

FINDING VALUE

There are three main ways to value real estate. Each is sensible, but no one method is right for every situation.

The most obvious approach is to find out what other properties comparable by size of unit or square feet or square metres sell for in the neighbourhood or in the city or town. Real estate agents are good sources of information. If a property is unusual in any way, then a premium or deduction should be calculated based on the cost of bringing a comparable property to a status similar to the one in question. The bottom line is that one should not get ahead of the market nor fall behind. Ultimately, one tries to bid below average, just as the seller wishes to have a price above average. The vendor or his or her agent may try to add spice to the asked price with hints that others are looking. Take your time. This is not the only way to establish the value of a property. You could say that this is a way of kicking the tires. It is quick, cheap, and incomplete.

The next approach in establishing value is to determine what it would cost to duplicate the property in question by construction. You have to add cost if the property needs to be upgraded and take off value if it is old and depreciated. These measures require a familiarity with buildings, codes, what trades charge, and what features can add to value. Professional property inspectors or appraisers are good sources of information for this approach.

> Your whole house is a speculative investment, the cost of which is reduced by the value of your occupancy, as though you pay yourself rent.

The last way of setting a value on a property for rent is to estimate what it will earn. The common measure is net operating income; that is, what the property will yield to the owner after costs including property taxes, relevant utilities, insurance charges, and estimated repairs. This number is net operating income. It can be raised over time if leases have escalator clauses and reduced for vacancy risk. If net operating income is, let's say, $100,000 a year before income tax and if the interest rate on a ten-year government bond is, say, 5 percent, then the base price of the property should be twenty times $100,000, or $2 million. That is the sum which, at 5 percent, would generate $100,000 a year. A commercial property is not as solid as a Government of Canada bond, so its price should reflect a higher return. To produce a 10 percent return, one would pay no more than $1 million. The value of this price estimation process is that it produces limits on what one can reasonably pay. If the cash flow from the property is $100,000 a year and you can buy it for $700,000, the yield would be 14 percent, a terrific deal. If the price at $3 million cuts the return of $100,000 to 3 percent, it is a poor deal unless a capital gain is a sure thing.

Is an investment in your home a good deal? On this point, one can find much disagreement. Some so-called experts say that money in your home is money which you have not invested. This is much too simple a point of view.

Let's say that you require 1,800 square feet to live comfortably. You have the $500,000 to buy it — just to keep things simple — but you have found a 3,000 square foot house with room for a basement suite or a granny apartment. If you lease space, the home can generate rental income. Moreover, even if the house cost, let's say, $4,000 a month to own and operate with mortgage interest and utilities, insurance, and so on, some part of the $4,000 and the opportunity cost of money in the down payment is a charge for your own occupancy. The remainder, if there is any, is a speculative real estate investment. Looked at the other way, the whole house is a speculative investment, the cost of which is reduced by the value of your occupancy. It is as though you pay yourself rent. That rent reduces the speculative component of ownership.

CONDO RISKS

Condominiums are a special situation in real estate investment. The price is whatever you pay, the mortgage and interest are negotiated, and then you move in. Over time, the condo participation payments, the monthly fees (called strata fees in B.C.), may rise. What was once a good deal can become a very costly deal.

What can happen is illustrated by the story of a co-op building at 2 Fifth Avenue in Manhattan. Occupants own shares in the co-op corporation. It's a condo concept with some New York twists. The fine, twenty-storey building has had distinguished owners like former mayor Ed Koch and the well-known playwright Larry Kramer. It also had old glazed bricks on the outside. The concept of glazing was that the ceramic coating would keep out water. But it did not. Instead, the bricks soaked up water and the glazing trapped it. There were nearly one million bricks in danger of falling, tons of mortar behind them, drains that did not work ... it had to be fixed. The building's board decided that all 289 units in the building would have to fork over US$30.7 million for the two-and-a-half-year job. It had to be done, for the risk to pedestrians below the wobbly bricks was undeniable. And it was done. The new bricks alone cost US$1.85 million. Then 270,000 pounds of steel supports had to be installed. Owners had to pay repair tabs averaging US$106,228 per owner, but nobody defaulted. This was Fifth Avenue, of course.[5]

It can turn out very differently if owners in a condo can't come up with the money. Assume that there are ten units in a condo. Assume that all are bought on high ratio mortgages so that the owners have just 5 percent or 10 percent of their initial price on the line. One owner can't afford payments on his or her unit and just leaves. Now the remaining nine owners have to pick up the cost. Their share of cost rises from 10 percent to 11.1 percent. Another moves out. Now the initial condo fee is up by 25 percent from what it was when there were ten occupants covering costs. The pressure is rising. Another two owners flee. Now there are six owners each forced to cover 167 percent of the original condo fees. If this keeps up, everybody will leave. Whether the owners are occupants or investors, the problem is the same. Those who are stuck with increased bills will either bite the bullet or put their units on the market at deep discounts. The remaining owners will inevitably suffer.

The problem of fleeing owners is most acute in condo developments with owners with mixed incomes. The lower income owners may not want to pay for improvements and prefer to let the development wither. The upper income owners want to put in major improvements and worry little about the cost. Lower income owners have to leave when faced with higher assessments. Either way, the development winds up with more risk and every owner has a greater chance of being wiped out by costs rising either with a fancy pool or by the process of having fewer pockets to pay the bills.

The astute investment property shopper will always ask why a unit is for sale. On this point, lawyer and investment maven Douglas Gray suggests that the motives of the seller should be examined. His list of reasons a property may be for sale include 1) inexperienced owner who hasn't enough time to handle details; 2) dispute among co-owners who prefer to sell and be done with the headache; 3) tax benefit if the property cannot be depreciated further; 4) capital gain appeals to owner; 5) the settling of an estate; 6) excessive cost of future repairs and maintenance; 7) too many vacancies; 8) problem of continuing financing; 9) owner's financial problems; 10) prices for the property are too good to pass up; and 11) general pessimism about a market or neighbourhood.[6] Needless to say, there can be a combination of these reasons, and when two or three are operating, the property and its value may go into a death spiral, with poor maintenance driving off owners and driving away potential buyers, tenants leaving, lenders demanding repayment, and lawyers acting for various interests adding their own bills.

THE ART OF RENTING

Condo tenants or tenants in a pure rental building can make the difference between a failed speculation and an investment that pays its own way. Selecting residential tenants is both science and art. The science lies in checking paperwork. The art is in talking to prospective tenants to get a sense of who they are. This is getting to know your customer and it is far more vital in forming a long-term relationship than it is for a shopper dropping into a store for a quick purchase. Needless to say, discrimination on the basis of race or religion or philosophical bent is illegal and unfair and can run up large lawyer bills.

Prospective tenants will bring a story about themselves: work, children, perhaps pets, and a potential history of downsizing or seeking larger space. The story needs to fit the situation. Landlords can obtain credit reports, but credit agencies have histories that should make even the most prudent of landlords or potential employers, for that matter, skeptical of report accuracy. Recent scandals of penetration of databases by hackers have exposed Equifax, formerly the Retail Credit Co. of Atlanta, Georgia, to scrutiny and much criticism. Credit agencies now use numerical scoring rather than gossip from neighbours, which was the credit reporting methodology many decades ago, but industry methods presume that those to be rated borrow for credit in ways which can be observed, and have employment and perhaps insurance and jobs and other indicia of conformity. If one fits the pattern, that's fine. Paradoxically, there are very wealthy and liquid people who do not fit, and people of modest means and no jobs who also pay bills, and rent in particular, on time. The bottom line is to judge the person and his or her story, not the paper trail.

The obvious question is from whence the prospective tenant comes. Check it out. Employment? Get a pay stub. Self-employment? Ask to see a tax return or a notice of assessment from the Canada Revenue Agency. Student? Get some university documentation such as a student card. If you do your own confirmation, you will have a sense of your tenant to be.

There are no guarantees of good conduct. Conduct within the law, such as a bit of noise, is a relationship problem. Brewing up illegal drugs would not be within the law and could lead to summary expulsion. You can find standard tenancy agreements at local stationers or online. They vary by province and territory. It will pay a prospective landlord to learn the details.

Some steps can make life easier for the landlord. Get a years' worth of postdated cheques. Obtain next of kin or good friend information — name, phones, emails, and so on. Make sure all parties know who pays the utilities, what the landlord's access to premises will be, and what payments will be charged for a bounced cheque or late payment, for pet poop, and for more than expected wear and tear. Before the tenant moves in, do a checklist of condition. Finally, use the golden rule for tenants: be good to the tenant, and he or she may be expected to respond in kind. If you act as a disciplinarian, you can expect friction and rebellion, complaints to government regulators, and even calls from lawyers. It is better to solve a problem over coffee and pie or whatever works than via hostile notes and emails. Oddly, the idea of avoiding adversarial relationships is seldom mentioned in books and online posts in tenant management.

TIME SHARES

Fractional ownership, alias time shares, is one of the most challenging forms of investment in property. Participation is often hyped by difficult-to-refuse invitations to parties, galas, freebie trips, buddy visits, and more. But think: If the time shares were so marvelous, why would promoters have to do somersaults to sell them?

The time share idea is that, for a fixed price, you get to use defined holiday properties or other units in a group for a modest additional cost or perhaps no extra charges whatever. The concept is to invest and enjoy. It does not always work that way.

Easy to get in but tough to get out of, there is often a poor aftermarket to sell shares. The promoter may buy them back at a huge discount. One can find resale services online, such as Secondary Ownership Group, which bills itself as Canada's Timeshare Resale Company.

See secondaryownershipgroup.ca and check for competing businesses. Getting more than one offer is simply good business.

Before you plunge, learn how your provincial or territorial laws cover rights to cancel. If you elect to buy while you are in Mexico or other jurisdictions and in some U.S. states, you may have no time or right to back out.[7] The downside of every time share is future commitment, for you will want to get your money's worth. Yet the promised use of other properties may hit a snag if they are not available when you want them. The best advice: check, investigate, and do your own detective work. If you find errors or defects in management or quality or if a time share company is besieged with lawsuits, be advised. Remember, there is usually more than one cockroach in the kitchen. Most of all, time shares, even when they are lovely to live in, are seldom good investments. Even if units are rented, costs of management can rise and your tastes may change. Locking into a deal with years or decades to run and no clear aftermarket that is known to work is capricious at best and foolish at worst.

If time shares are so marvelous, why do promoters have to do somersaults to sell them?

PRICE CYCLES

Real estate prices move in cycles. Easily said, but the hard part is identifying the cycles and measuring their effect on quantities and prices of various sorts of properties. The shorter the holding period, the more important it is to get the cycle stages right. If you plan to buy and hold for a few decades, it hardly matters. But few investors in real estate have decades in mind.

The most important cycle is what the broader economy is doing. If the economy goes into recession, investors will tend to buy less and may have to sell assets to raise cash so they can pay off loans granted by newly nervous bankers and investment dealers eager to ensure that clients do not run off and leave their brokerages or banks holding the bag. As gross domestic product changes go from rising at a few percent a year to stagnant or worse, property prices fall. That happened in 2008 and 2009, when investors rushed to sell what they could, homes in the U.S. were financed with mortgages their owners, many unemployed, could not service, and even solid commercial properties went begging for buyers.

There are also local business cycles that reflect immigration of workers to rapidly growing cities; fleeing residents as local business contracts (a feature of the boom/bust Alberta market), self-generated urban decay (the American rust belt is an example), and rapid growth when major new industries open plants.

For an investor, the problem is to understand, map, and then time these cycles. It is a huge task, but to ignore the problem is more foolish than trying to manage it. Realtors will say they have a handle on cycles, and some may indeed be able to marshal their experience to the advantage of potential buyers. But realtors' loyalties are often divided, and many want to get a sale done and make their commissions. Talking to many brokers and to independent mortgage brokers as well can add to your understanding. Indeed, if you are going to put six or seven figures on the line, it is foolish not to seek the advice of these market watchers. Given that property investing almost always has longer holding periods than investing in financial assets like stocks, bonds, options, and so on, property is more like a marriage with an asset than a fling with a stock. Most of all, remember that property is always local, unlike trading shares of Royal Bank that are the same in Vancouver as they are in Montreal.

THE COST OF TIME

There are two roads to property investing. One is buying real estate directly. You tie up a good deal of money; have to pay for legal services; and may have to pay for site appraisal, surveys, investigations if all bills have been paid by the owner, legal fees, and title transfer costs. You wind up with a tangible asset and then have to buy some level of insurance from fire and windstorm to comprehensive coverage. The only way to get diversification is to buy more property, leveraging equity in the first property to provide a down payment for the next.

All of this takes a good deal of time, though one would expect that time per deal would diminish with experience. You can spend less time on deals and get exposure to more types of property — apartments, office towers, shopping centres — by putting money into real estate investment trusts, REITs for short. You are then at the end of the line for payment after secured lenders, for example, and you do not own a tangible asset. But you have diversification, low costs, and no need to spend time as a property detective or, for that matter, shovelling snow for your tenants.

> You can spend less time on deals and get exposure to more types of property by putting money into real estate investment trusts.

REAL ESTATE INVESTMENT TRUSTS AND MORTGAGE INVESTMENT CORPORATIONS

The concept of REITs is simple: a company assembles many properties in a holding company, which passes income through to unitholders after deduction of costs. They exist in many countries and have been part of the Canadian investment landscape since 1993. The upside is professional management of numerous properties. The downside is that unitholders are at the end of the line of folks who get paid. Employees, secured lenders, and suppliers get paid long before unitholders.

REITs are as much part of the stock market as they are part of the real estate market. Because their units trade every moment of every day, their prices change minute by minute. At present, shopping centre specialty REITs are down while apartment REITs and those REITs that specialize in office buildings are up. There are other ways to buy commercial property on the stock market. Brookfield Asset Management Inc., for example, generated an impressive 118.47 percent return for the five years ended May 30, 2018. It is large and diversified, and its price has about doubled in the period. But Artis Real Estate Investment Trust, which also has office buildings, is down 12.26 percent in the same period. Each play is different, while all focus on the cost of borrowed money in a market in which interest rates are widely expected to rise to something like their long-term average of 5 percent for ten-year government bonds from about half that when this chapter was written.

Mortgage investment corporations (MICs) are alternative lenders. Set up as private companies and by builders who want to take in money from the public to finance their projects, they lend less than banks' 80 percent of a project's cost and tend to take on risks higher than those acceptable to banks. Their returns have recently been as much as 8 percent to 12 percent, but for that kind of money, investors have to accept illiquidity — money may be stuck for five years. Some MICs are very small operations, some larger. On the whole, MICs are property lenders that provide no tangible asset such as a building and no capital gains. The investors in MICs are not property owners. Their risks are high, for in addition to the default risk intrinsic in any business loan, there are no secondary markets for investors in most private mortgage pools. The only way out is through redemption of units by the pools under varying arrangements. Some MICs ask their investors, really lenders, 90 days following a request for money. Other MICs allow redemption on only a few days of the year, and then only after notice to withdraw has been given. The majority of mortgage pools are not publicly traded, so there are few ways out before redemption.

MIC investments are relatively high-risk commitments. What seems a good deal — high income from what is often a small company holding many mortgages — is usually a narrow sector bet on loans to developers who can't get money at lower rates from a bank or other mainline lender. For investors who accept that level of risk, there are alternatives that provide a competitive level of income and risk. For example, high-yield bonds have secondary markets for resale and often have daily pricing through specialized boards that investment dealers can access, and their issuers publish annual and quarterly financial reports that allow holders to see what their money is doing. To be sure, some MICs also provide accessible documentation. But high-yield corporate bonds are more liquid. From our point of view, the negatives of MICs outweigh the positives. Be advised and be warned.

HOW TANGIBLE DO YOU WANT?

The final variable in real estate investment is one's taste for tangible assets, which any house or condo certainly is, or for the abstraction of shares of companies or units of funds that follow managers' ideas, as mutual funds do, or indices, as exchange traded funds do.

The downside of tangible real estate is maintenance. There can be calls from tenants at night to fix the plumbing, charges of noncompliance by rent review boards and perhaps investigations by health departments, tenant damage, vacancy, late payments, and inability to evict deadbeats until after months of nonpayment, and sometimes in some places never in the dead of winter.

The upside of property investment is the use of leverage to achieve high rates of return on equity, the ability of the owner to use one equity in one property to secure another, and the certainty that as one learns to manage a real estate portfolio, growth of capital is almost — but not quite — certain.

The concluding word and wisdom of real estate investing is that homes for rent that are mostly or fully paid, in good shape, and with good tenants are largely immune from the mayhem of the business cycle. Rising interest rates have no direct effect if the mortgage is largely or fully paid. What happens to bank stocks or shares in steel or pharmaceuticals, insurance or car parts won't matter. In extreme meltdowns, such as that of 2008, there will be spillover effects. But the rental property will come through intact, there will be a tenant in place or another ready to rent, and income flow won't suffer much if at all.

Even for investors who don't like the relative intimacy of renting a home compared to the perfectly nonhuman process of buying stocks online or even through an investment dealer, having some real estate exposure makes sense. To have no real estate exposure through actual ownership of property or ownership of companies that own property is foolish if one wishes to have a diversified portfolio. Only the degree of closeness to an actual building and tenants with heartbeats is in question.

CHAPTER 7

Mistakes: Turning Bad Experiences into Assets

As any decision maker knows, mistakes are part of the process of investing; indeed, of life itself. You can boil them down to mistakes of omission, tactical errors, defects in knowledge and understanding, and, finally, errors from the grab bag of failing to know what is not knowable. The list of what can and often does go wrong urges a sense of humility on investors. The wise investor prepares for error. First, however, error has to be defined.

Capital markets are agnostic on what is right and what is wrong. Moreover, there is no definition of an investing error. It can be picking the wrong company; unfortunate timing, which is a tactical error on the buy or on the sell or both; picking the wrong industry or country; or, for quantitative investors or others who trust in charts above all else, picking the wrong wobbles — the so-called technicians' words for a certain pattern. For other investors who seek stocks with sound fundamentals or shorts who like unsound fundamentals or just good companies with over-priced shares, it can be putting too much emphasis on price or earnings or sales or enterprise value or scores of other measures. This is mistaking numbers for understanding and knowledge. Finally, there is market volatility and fresh negative information that has not been anticipated. That's the unknowable.

Knowing, in the sense of investing, starts with being able to separate what is probably right from probably wrong. If it's your business that's concerned, you have a seat-of-the-pants idea of what works and what does not. In the distant realm of capital markets, investors tend to take the word of others whose motives are often to sell stocks and bonds. They get paid and shift risk to the investor.

> It is said that time heals all, and for patient investors who buy and hold, that is mostly true.

The path to profit is a bridge across this chasm of hazards. The market is largely a kettle of unknowns in the very short run or minutes, hours, and a few days. In the long run of years and decades, good sense and economics rule. In the middle of this timing span, periods of a few months to a few years, the investor must focus on what matters and exclude from view what does not. It is a demanding task, for in every case the investor must examine other peoples' businesses and get a sense of what makes them tick. It is far from the organic sense of the small business owner who knows their enterprise intimately.

It is said that time heals all, and for patient investors who buy and hold, that is mostly true. Individual companies come and go, but industries tend to survive particular companies and, moreover, entire markets can survive collapse of businesses, industries, and even political regimes.

It is also said that reward rises with risk. That is true, but one may need to buy hundreds of stocks and hold them for many decades to see the results of betting on the nastiest stocks or the riskiest bonds on the theory that they will reward investors in the end. Few small investors have the fortitude or the cash or even the lifespan to confirm the linkage of time and trend. Our own time frame is seldom more than a decade. After all, a small business would struggle if in the red for a few years. A decade is the longest time we would ask any investor to wait for a concept to work or a market to recover.

With all that said, the idea of a mistake has to be seen as fluid and relative. There are few absolutes, other than bankruptcy of a company once thought sound or the horror of a short investor who finds that the stock he thought hopeless is rising into the stratosphere, perhaps driving the investor into insolvency.

The core problem of investing in any asset or class of assets is that prices have a way of being alarmingly volatile. The French geophysicist Didier Sornette, whose book on financial fluctuations, *Why Stock Markets Crash: Critical Events in Complex Financial Systems*,[1] is a landmark in measuring the depth and frequency of market blowouts, points out that "a daily return amplitude of more than 4 percent should be typically observed only once in 63 years, while a return amplitude of more than 5 percent should never be seen in our limited history. The New York Stock Exchange drop of 22.6 percent on October 19, 1987, and the rebound of 9.7 percent on October 21, 1987, are abnormal,... They are essentially impossible. The fact that they occurred tells us that the market can deviate significantly from the norm."[2] Even with some manipulation of the normal bell curve — and financial markets do not have "normal" curves — the drop in 1987 should not happen more than once in 520 million years, Sornette says. His point is that stock markets are not "normal" in a statistical sense. The reasons, of course, are investors' hopes, fears, and a world of unexpected forces. In statistical terms, the amplitude — that is, the severity and frequency of major declines — is greater than a notion of independent, uncorrelated events would suggest. Psychology, which in a market decline means fear, drives the numbers. The task for the investor is to know major drops are inevitable. Courage, you may say, has to go with analysis.

A MATTER OF EXPECTATIONS

Thus, our view of what is good or bad is mostly relative to expectations. A rotten stock bought cheaply enough can be a terrific investment. Yet a company bought at the height of optimism for its future can turn out to be a loser when its earnings languish. What is a profound error in the short run may be a trifle in the long run. It follows that a short run winner may become a loser in time.

Crummy companies can make great investments, and great companies can make for terrible investments. At the end of the day, investing in stocks or bonds or real estate or farmland is about future income. If you overpay for this future income, you will probably be disappointed.

For instance, you can buy Salesforce.com. The technology and the value to the end client is nearly infinite. For the client, Salesforce is a great company. However, the stock has traded for 229 times last year's earnings or 75 times next year's. Clearly, the company is growing … but is one willing to pay effectively decades into the future's worth of earnings? A lot can change in a decade.

Think of early computer makers, like Commodore International, that have long since bitten the digital dust. Commodore sold millions of its market-leading C64 computer in the early 1980s, but it filed for bankruptcy in April 1994. Its technology was surpassed by other computer makers. In little more than a decade, it went from leader to follower to dead. What makes the case interesting is how fast it happened. The lesson: Don't believe that cycles in technology run on the same clock as those in more banal industries.

The problem of buying into technologies or market enthusiasms comes down to the question of what an investment is worth. Put another way, how much money do you want to pay to take a flyer on an idea? Not every investment can pay a profit in its early years, but without earnings and dividends, a company and its shares are far riskier than shares of a business with dependable earnings and a dividend long paid and well supported by earnings. The risks of going from the known and solid to the unknown and relatively chancy are huge.

"One of my clients asked that I buy Tesla, maker of electric cars," Benoit Poliquin recalls. "Tesla is innovative and its chief is visionary. The concept of the electric car is environmentally right. But as an investment, Tesla, as of the day of writing, has no earnings and dividends, yet it has a market capitalization — that's number of shares multiplied by the share price — of US$54 billion. Compare that to Ford Motor Company, which has a market cap of US$49 billion and a conservative p/e of 7, and Fiat Chrysler, which has a market cap of US$37 billion and a modest ratio of price to earnings of 6.0."

Tesla may be the future and turning out gas guzzlers may be the past, but Ford and GM, among others, make electric cars and hybrids. Electric cars are not a unique technology, in other words. Tesla sells about

200,000 cars a year, while Fiat Chrysler sells that many in a month just in the United States. Tesla is losing US$300 million each year, while Fiat Chrysler has a profit of over US$9 billion. Tesla may be the future, but at the moment it is an expensive bet on a technology that it does not control. The better investment is the established auto industry, which pays dividends and actually has earnings that can go into a p/e ratio. In future, Tesla, which has a negative p/e at the time of writing, may turn a profit. Then it will be a potential investment.

Time is everything and ignorance is the enemy. The problem of knowing the future is that, as the author Nicholas Nassim Taleb has said, "What we don't know is more important than what we do know."[3] These unknown unknowns are the black swans he made famous based on the discovery in the nineteenth century that swans, always thought to be white, were actually black in Australia.

> The problem of buying into market enthusiasm comes down to an investment's worth: how much do you want to pay to take a flyer on an idea?

The essence of his argument that unexpected events cannot be foreseen is that there is no reasonable way to make bets on them.

The largest events exceed our perspective. Taleb's point rests on what we have now that did not exist or could not have been anticipated hundreds of years ago — travel by airplane, high-speed data transfer, television, electronic banking, and our level of medical science. His final point: The big stuff is not just beyond prediction, it is also beyond imagination. The existence of cell phones and the sagas of such makers as Motorola and Nokia, Apple and Samsung, the death rattles of chemical imaging and the resulting shrivelling of Eastman Kodak — it was impossible to predict, even to conceive, in 1960; imaginable, but not with much credibility, in 1980; and done and ancient history today. The implication is that it is not an investor's fault not to know the future. But prudence suggests ranking one's risks and allocating money on what is likely, and keeping a reserve of money, a cash balance or liquid bonds, for what is not likely.

In terms of our daily investing, it is said that who wins the game depends on where the goal posts are set. On timing, setting the goal posts is everything, for if the starting post for a volatile stock is set at a time when shares are low and the end post is set when they are high, the investment performance measured will be grand. If the posts are set when the stock is high on the theory that it will go higher, but then it reverts to a lower value, performance will seem poor. Over periods of many decades, the goal post problem recedes. In ten-year spans, it still matters. Twenty-year spans, too. At forty and fifty years, it no longer matters very much.[4] But mortality and patience usually confine the investor to seeing spans in no more than two decades. Unfortunately, most private investors have neither the patience nor, in many cases, the lifespan to wait out the periods of short- to mid-term volatility.

ERRORS OF KNOWLEDGE AND UNDERSTANDING

When you buy an investment, say a commercial rental building, you seek profit. This profit will come from the rental income less the operating and financing charges each month and the appreciation of the land on which the building sits. We can all agree that buildings depreciate. In fact, the tax authorities recognize this immutable truth by allowing for tax breaks on the depreciation.

Many rookie investors have no knowledge of this, much less the understanding. Seasoned investors will look at the condition of the elevators; the HVAC system; the condition of the lobby; the roof; the outside walls' masonry, paint, or cladding; and even the parking lot to assess the value of the building. What they are doing here is a due diligence exercise to gain an understanding of the future investment the building will require. From this assessment, they will understand how much the building will need in the future in terms of further investments. The present value of these future costs should be deducted from the current value of the building. From the curb, the knowledgeable investor with experience in property management can make good assessments. All the private investor considering a wager on a property company like Brookfield Asset Management Inc. can do is to appraise the executives and study the books.

The importance of timing cannot be overestimated. It can make losers of winners and winners of losers. It can make timing an exercise in wisdom fulfilled or hope dashed. In very short time periods, say a day or a week, most stocks will just wobble a bit. If you buy a chartered bank and expect your investment to double, you will surely be disappointed. If you instead buy a volatile commodity with borrowed money, a weekly 25 percent move in the underlying asset doubled by a 50 percent loan could get you a 50 percent gain with a corresponding risk of loss. But an investment in a drudge stock or sluggish index that gains only 2 percent a year could double in three decades.

It comes down to a matter of knowing what you want or, put another way, why you are making a commitment of the past, which really means your savings, to a future idea such as profit or a dividend stream. An investor with a short time horizon, a few months or a year, may plunk down money to buy a quick capital gain. Another may be patient and just wait for dividends. The difference is the time of delivery.

ERROR OF UNKNOWN UNKNOWNS

Several years ago, Andrew Allentuck bought preferred shares of a world-class mining company that had been beaten down by falling ore prices. "I was sure they could pay the dividend that would be due. Just weeks after I had bought shares at a handsome discount from the issue price, the company was taken over by a larger mining concern. They paid off the shares at full redemption price, denying me the dividend stream and instead flinging a large capital gain at me."

Was Allentuck wrong to make the investment? "Yes, I had ignored the potential for takeover. Did I suffer? Not really. The capital gain got reinvested and it eventually raised the income I had wanted in the first place."

You could say that this little tale of a happy outcome shows some sort of investing skill, but in a more demanding environment, say a portfolio managed for a defined return in a specified time, his good luck would have been a reason to be fired. Luck is not the same thing as an intended result, though they can be mistaken for each other. Goals can be specified and written down. In a short time, they can be realized or not, measured and recorded. Over longer periods, such as the years required to harvest dividends, it can be hard to distinguish success from a mistake. In the end, whether one succeeds or fails as an investor is about the goal posts. In a short period, a few months or perhaps a few years, success or failure can be readily ascertained. Over periods of decades, the goals can blur. A tidy profit in a boom is merely what is expected. The same profit taken when markets are disintegrating may seem miraculous.

HOW DIVERSIFIED ARE INDEXES?

On the theory of diversification, the Morgan Stanley Capital International World Index ETF (XWD) should be the most stable of indices. And yet this global index is cap weighted. Thus the U.S. has 52 percent of the weight as of summer, 2018, Japan has about 8 percent, the U.K. 6 percent, and Canada 3 percent — the same as France, Germany, and Switzerland, each 3 percent. No investor could keep all the stocks in his or her head, but it has returned a total of about 600 percent since March 2003.

The MSCI index's phenomenal return comes with a cost in volatility, for it has a 14 percent annual standard deviation. So, the investor has had to live with returns that were up an average 36 percent in the good years and down 20 percent on average in bad years, with a few years when the swoon was as much as 50 percent. Paradoxically, if you measure the long-run returns from good years like August 2000, the gain is just 2.8 percent per year compounded. If you measure from August 1987, the return is 5.95 percent. What is the right measuring period? Larry Berman, co-founder of ETF Capital Management and a Chartered Financial Analyst, suggests that the problem in taking the long view is "recency bias"; that is, the tendency to discount the distant past in favour of the immediate future.[5] Ultimately, the problem is one of faith in markets and oneself, for when you buy what you know, the problem of statistical inference of the past to the present diminishes.

It is clear that the goal-post problem and the concept of error that accompanies seemingly bad-timing decisions recedes as the period of time measured lengthens. There is more time to succeed and, given that inflation tends over time to drive up asset prices and, therefore, stock returns, most investments over periods of many years should be able to trick a profit.

THE COST OF CONVICTION

In short periods, for day traders, catching the top and bottom of what are often just random price changes is almost impossible. It would be like making perfect moves in roulette — picking the number on which the ball lands — twice in a row. The odds against that with thirty-six spots on the table and a top zero are 1/37 squared. A triple play would have odds of one in 50,653. No wonder a lot of players just go for red or black.

The stock market, in spite of catastrophic crashes, is more forgiving than the roulette wheel. Over a period of years, time and inflation tend to separate lows from highs. Buying and holding a broad index fund or well-diversified portfolio for a few decades is almost certain to be rewarding, with two caveats. One, it has to be a good index. The S&P 500 would be fine. The Nikkei 225, which hit a peak on December 29, 1989, at 38,958, was at 22,539 on June 5, 2018, just 58 percent of that peak after almost three decades of stagnation — not a good example of the buy-and-hold principle. One can add that bets on the Tsarist railway bonds in 1913 (defaulted) or German industrials in 1939 on the eve of World War II (many later seized by Allies; some corporation heads prosecuted for war crimes) would have been exceptions to the idea of inevitable recovery.

> In short periods, catching the top and bottom of what are often just random price changes is almost impossible, like making perfect moves in roulette.

The risk of error grows with the volatility of the stock, bond, or option. Stock volatility is measured by beta, which is just the bounciness of a stock in relation to the market's bounciness. A stock with a beta of 1 has the same volatility as the market. At 2, it is twice as jumpy. Bond volatility tends to grow as the quality of the bond declines. Junk bonds are, therefore, more volatile on a short-term basis than investment grade bonds. And the longer the term of the bond, the more interest payments will seem great or awful. Therefore, the prices of thirty-year bonds are more volatile than those of one-year bonds.

OPTIONS

Option pricing is a field and career of its own. Option investing and option pricing are targeted to take advantage of the intrinsic volatility of underlying asset prices. Options are always bets on the asset going up or down within a specified time period. To do it right, you have to calculate or guess the future price and the time frame or, for European options, the precise expiry date when it is going to happen.

Options are a zero-sum game — winnings of some precisely equal losses of others on fundamentals, and less than zero-sum after trading costs such as commissions and fees. That means that the sum of all bets is more than the sum of all payoffs. The difference is what intermediaries make. There are speculators: buyers of options, defined as the right but not the obligation to buy (call) or sell (put) a stock will make profitable prediction. The prediction has to be correct not only on the direction, but also the amplitude, the strike price, and the time to expiry. The speculator has to get both the time and the target price or target range right.

The seller of the option is effectively the casino. Time is on his or her side because options decay to a value of $0 by expiry date. Studies have shown that up to 70 percent of options expire worthless. Sellers of options seldom win big, but they do not often lose big either when properly structured (hedged). Many players are known as "grinders." They will grind their way to higher earnings by capturing the high probabilities that the speculators will not see their trifecta bets on time, asset price direction, and value of stake come in for them.

Moreover, if returns arrive in lumps rather than streams, you may think you are wrong, but actually be right in the long run. The clock does not forgive the impatient. Best bet: Temper fear of loss with advice. It's not that the person you consult will know the future, but that thinking through a question or issue will illuminate the risks and rewards of getting in or out.

In the end, it is not so much absolute judgment of the worth of a stock that makes or breaks an investment concept. It is the time frame in which the investment is supposed to move. Assets with infinite life expectancies thus cannot make prophets or liars out of patient people.

Those assets that are tied to clocks or calendars can turn the wisest of people into fools.

Time is a proxy for other variables that make an investment a winner or a dreadful mistake. Consider the fate of Ford Motor Co. Priced at US$37.07 on January 3, 1998, shares slumped to US$1.87 at the beginning of 2009, about where they traded at the beginning of 1980. They traded at US$11.30 at the end of June 2018. Investors who were short Ford in early 1998 could have made a fortune. Those who were long in January 1998 have yet to see a profit.

> In most cases, save global cataclysms such as 2008, when one market falls, another rises.

EXPECTATION AND DIVERSIFICATION

Mistakes are defined as errors of expectation or knowledge and understanding of the future. A sustainable dividend flow can cover a lot of errors in a stock purchase, just as reinvesting interest coupons from a slumping bond will make up for the interest the bond investor does not get from new bonds as interest rates rise.

Diversification also reduces the timing problem. The ups and downs of the shares of a single company tend to exceed the volatility of its industry, and the bounces of the industry shares expressed as an index will tend to be higher than that of its market. One market tends to wobble more than all markets in the world. The investor who wants to minimize the irregularity of returns characteristic of individual stocks, industries, and national markets can buy international blend indexes such as the MSCI World Index. If you buy this one for all the right reasons, only a global recession is likely to derail it. It will not be headache-free, for it will reflect global trends. In theory, however, it should be very forgiving of timing errors. In most cases, other than global cataclysms such as 2008, when one market falls, another rises. To say nothing of currency moves. One can never lose sight of American shares nor the value of the U.S. dollar against other currencies. But with money spread all over the place, a bad day or month in New York is not necessarily fatal. Moreover, a broad index makes even fuzzy goals and imperfect outcomes seem acceptable. A year's tidy profit of 8 percent, after all, is nice compensation for the sin of failing to achieve the goal of a 9 percent return.

ERRORS OF OMISSION

Errors of omission can be quite subtle. For example, one can predict that the electrification of the world's car fleet is inevitable. However, how does one invest to profit from this prospect? One may think the thing to do is to buy the dominant maker of electric cars or the battery makers.

If the past is a guide, this might prove to be a mistake. New technology companies are in a constant state of new investments. They depend on injections of fresh investor capital. When enough investors believe their story, the stock goes up.

Wise investors remember history. Any technology is dominated by leaders who are usually replaced or die off. Think of any new technology and their leaders of the day. Chances are, they are no longer around.

A better approach is to avoid the trap of buying the first inventors or appliers of new technologies. One can cash in on new technologies by buying into the supply chain. For example, electric cars will need parts such as transmissions, new technologies, special tires, and new materials both inside and out. Plants will have to be built, dealerships modified, and a new way to service these products designed.

In conclusion, you can spot a trend and find ways to invest in it. But you must also widen your focus to include winners that supply inputs to the new technology, as well as those that will lose out from the acceptance of the new technology. Not doing so is an error of omission.

The ultimate question for any investor in stocks, bonds, and, for that matter, almost any other asset is whether the system or their part of it is stable. If all prices are stable and stay in perfect synchronization with underlying corporate earnings and net worth, other companies' earnings, and so on, then there can be no speculative gains. There would be no uncertainty to bet on. All returns would be in the nature of interest paid for postponing spending.

The real world is not like that. Stability is at best a concept. In reality, companies may borrow heavily to the point that all future earnings are pledged as collateral. Then there is nothing left for stockholders. This "Minsky Moment," named after the late economist Hyman Minsky, has been used to explain the Russian debt crisis and bond default in 1998 and, of course, the 2008 mortgage derivative calamity.[6] Overextended investors hit with margin calls see their balance sheets crumble. They may rush to sell and add fuel to the fire of asset declines, forcing even more sales and making bad situations even worse. If there are no bids available, prices tumble to where the wise or the courageous move into the market to snap up bargains. It can be a painful adjustment.

> Diversification is usually understood to mean putting money on different assets, but the word has a timing implication as well.

Investors who do not see these great waves coming, the embodiment of Taleb's black swan, can only adopt a strategy that gives value to what they know and minimizes the damage from what they do not know.

We need to make a distinction here between solid value that endures and market value. We'll call the first embedded value. It is the correlate of what a shopkeeper knows about his business and his customers. Market value is changeable. It depends on the popularity of a stock, market fashions, passing moments of fear and greed, what analysts say, and even street gossip. Dot-coms were fashionable; now they are not.

John Maynard Keynes, whose concepts for using debt to jump start depressed economies still prevail, once said, "When I get new information, I may change my mind." That is a reasonable statement. Applied to investing, the question becomes: If my strategy is not working, should I stick it out or change it? In other words, go with the mistake of the moment, or try something else?

If stock prices merely oscillate in symmetric harmony, then there is not much risk in waiting. If the oscillations are not symmetric, one may have to try something different. The old saying that even a broken clock is right twice a day applies to the first situation but not to the second.

It comes down to asking whether one should learn from mistakes or stick with a theory that should be right. If you have 200 chances to flip coins for heads and none appear in the first 100, do you bet heavily on toss 101 on the basis that heads have to start turning up? Or do you stick to a 50/50 bet that each flip of a perfect coin is independent?

The best answer is the second. Each toss is independent, and the chances of tosses 101 and 151 and 199 out of 200 turning up heads are equal to each other. If the coins are perfect, then, applied to stock picking, you should stick to a given strategy.

This is not to say that picking coins is the only way to approach risk. There is also the question of how much to bet. And now we move to diversification strategy as a control for winning and losing.

Diversification is usually understood to mean putting money on different assets, but the word has a timing implication as well. The chances of absolute loss are high in short time periods for major stocks with broad product mixes. If you buy Royal Bank for a 5 percent gain on price including any dividend payable and your hold period is a week, the odds are strong that you will lose money after trading fees. If you buy the stock for a 5 percent total return in five years, you are almost certain to come out in the black, especially if you add in the dividends you will have been paid.

MANAGING VOLATILITY

The odds are different for bonds, for the clock is always ticking. Ten years is a conventional bond horizon, though one can buy shorter bonds, often called bills, for a day or ten days or a year. As well, there are long bonds with maturities stretching out to thirty years or even longer. No matter what the lifespan of the bond, as maturity approaches, the bond should trend toward its redemption price. Ten years out or thirty years for U.S. Treasury or Government of Canada bonds, expectations of rising or falling inflation, or, in the case of corporate bonds, credit worries, can send the bonds soaring or swooning.

In mid-2016, with Japanese, German, and Swiss government bonds priced so high that their redemption prices were less than their market prices — thus assuring a loss — any perception of returning inflation was likely to drop some of these bonds by 10 percent or even more. Bonds, once the steadiest and most boring of investments, became casino games and, by contrast, large cap stocks assumed the steadiness of bonds. Bonds were being held for capital gains, stocks for income. It is the inverted world of Alice dropped into the rabbit hole.

Given that it is time that determines success or failure and allowing for the possibility that anything can happen before the clock is up,
what parameters should an investor use for targeting gains? Our answer
depends on the asset class. For very volatile assets, say commodities, a
long-run view may be irrelevant. Coal was once a fundamental asset. The
big producers are gone or headed into bankruptcy. The implication is that
investing with a thirty- or fifty-year, not to say hundred-year, horizon is
a fantasy of permanence. Even over shorter periods, corporate morbid-
ity can lack the best laid plans. For example, of the five hundred largest
companies in the United States in 1957, only seventy-four were still part
of that select group, the S&P 500, at the turn of the twenty-first century. A
few had been merged. The rest had dropped out as they'd shrivelled, shut
down voluntarily, or were put out of business by creditors.[7]

The largest mistake, and perhaps one that is inevitable, is failure to
see ahead. It is difficult to anticipate catastrophes that have not happened, much less to time them. The small stuff, such as occasional market meltdowns, are a sure thing. But could one have anticipated the
market-breaking crisis of September 11, 2001? The New York Stock
Exchange closed for a week until September 17, the longest shut-
down since 1933. On the first day of trading after 9/11, the market fell
684 points, a 7.1 percent drop, which was the biggest loss for one trading
day in the NYSE's history. Markets recovered, of course, but no one other
than the perpetrators of the 9/11 atrocity could have timed the event
nor estimated its consequences.

Economists call the 9/11 attack "exogenous"; that is, having a source
outside the economic system. What to do to prepare for another event,
perhaps not that kind of tragedy, but a gigantic earthquake in the west-
ern part of North America — long since predicted but not dated? The
conventional answer is to have a lot of cash. An unconventional answer
is to invest in commodities that would be in short supply if the economic
system shut down. Or buy gold or gold certificates. More radical but fashionable in some circles is to buy ammo and canned soup. Each of these
answers is a form of diversification. One can add that investing in foreign
markets would also help.

It is possible to buy a kind of portfolio insurance by diverging from
strict price targets to price plus dividend or, for investors who like to earn

investment income while waiting for prices to rise, by adjusting a price target for income from selling covered calls; that is, the right of another investor to take your stock if the price rises above the call price.

Our final word on errors is that one should always avoid situations where, your back to the wall, selling is essential. That happens when you get a margin call to pay up — often when a stock has dropped a good deal. Having a hefty cash reserve, the higher the better as stock risk rises, is essential. Second best is a line of credit at your bank, but if you are overleveraged, it can lead to loss not just of a stock, but of a home, too. The worst of all tactics is to double down; that is, to buy more of a stock or other asset on the theory that it will bounce up at least as much as it has declined, thus cancelling out the loss or perhaps making more of the loss.

Doubling down as a theory has a long history. In eighteenth-century France, it was called a Martingale. Intuitively, if you double your bets on even odds, eventually you should win. Unfortunately, it does not work that way because the bet size increases exponentially, and, in the end, if you do win, your total return is the sum of all bets made less all losses. If you start with one dollar and lose four times, you will have bet $1 + $2 + $4 + 8 = $15 and, on the next bet, you put down $16, then win. Your $32 win, less lost bets less the $16 capital on the final bet makes $32. Take off your $16 stake, which is returned to you, and you have a gain of $16 less $15 lost. Your prize is $1. Given that you can have an infinite string of losses, you can run out of money before you win. Indeed, statistical evidence shows that long strings of losses are more common than gamblers imagine.

On the other hand, buying more of a stock after it has fallen on the theory that things have changed and you recognize the change for the better quicker than the market could, in theory, work to your advantage. However, the market is efficient and there are many astute players out there. Our feeling on this point — and feeling it is, for there is no conclusive evidence for the rightness or wrongness of buying more on the idea that if you like something at $20, you should like it twice as much when you can have it for $10 — is that rather than try to win back a loss, you should diversify to something else. Diversification is both insurance for error and a payback mechanism if you do err. That's a better plan than doubling down — special circumstances excepted.

We come back to the idea of understanding a portfolio as well as a small merchant knows their business. In a sense, it comes down to both honesty with oneself and getting the balance of optimism and pessimism just right.

There is enough data published every day, enough advice accompanying it, price and market forecasts, statistical studies linking variables, confessions of losers, boasts of winners, academic papers, and news stories to overwhelm anyone who wants to keep up with it. One must be selective, but the very act of selection of others' thoughts and research is biased. It may be hard to make the right choice every time, picking the advice that will get you the profits you expect, but it is relatively easy to identify what is downright stupid and avoid it.

> It may be hard to pick advice that will get you profits, but it is relatively easy to identify what is downright stupid.

TWELVE DUMB IDEAS

What is will be. Profits will continue or losses will continue. This is linear, unidirectional thinking, and it has little basis. Things change, and many portfolios that lose money one year turn out to do very well the next. The past is prologue, but no more. In an investment sense, a drop in an asset price may be reason to buy, just as a rise might be reason to sell. One can make the comparison with tomatoes — buy cheap, sell dear — but stocks and bonds have a different sense to most people. Cheapness alone is not an adequate reason to buy. It comes down to one's ability to squeeze a tomato and the harder task of analyzing a security.

1. **High values for a stock or bond must be right. The crowd drives value, so don't fight it. Join in.** The truth is that momentum investing, buying on a price trend rather than fundamentals, is a way to lose money. Remember Bre-X, which issued every higher profit forecasts each week that suckers lined up to buy? There was no gold at all. It was hype feeding hype. Nortel Networks as the centre of the digital world?

Enron — a pure fraud. Each was a stock market darling until the truth emerged, shocking analysts who were aboard and afraid to rock the boat. Do your own digging. The biggest mistake an investor can make is to take the word of an "expert," especially one paid by an investment dealer to whip up interest in the stock.

2. **Cheap stocks are worthless.** No, not necessarily. Some are deservedly cheap, but others are just ignored, not understood, or have intrinsic value not reflected by price. Typically, the cheap but golden stock will have an asset that is not well valued or vast sums of cash in the bank. There is no substitute for reading financial statements, especially the footnotes.

3. **Companies with soaring earnings are great.** Sometimes, yes. But earnings management, the accounting bag of tricks for slowing costs or accelerating sales, can turn a sick dog of a company into a pedigreed star. Read the income statements and be sure that earnings changes are roughly in parallel with sales changes, and that accounts receivable are not rising — if customers don't pay, there may be good reason.

4. **Rising returns are good.** Well, yes, they can be. But if they are the result of taking on more loans, stressing balance sheets, those earnings just reflect more risk. You want to know why returns are rising. Sometimes it's just because managers fiddle them in order to raise their bonuses.

5. **Linkages are benevolent.** As interest rates fell from 1983 to 2017, with few exceptions, investors paid ever more to get declining income from bonds and ever more for stocks that paid attractive dividends or did not. The idea behind quantitative easing used by many central banks from 2009 onward was to make fixed income less attractive and equity risk in stocks or any direct business investment more attractive. It helped to prolong the bond boom to ridiculous levels. On an equity comparison, a $1,000 government bond that pays 1.2 percent per year or $12 has an equivalent p/e of 83. Yet that was the going rate for ten-year bonds. The income did not cover inflation and would not rise. Similarly, so-so

mid-cap and small cap stocks, especially in emerging markets, flourished as investors scrambled for any kind of
return. When interest rates rise, overpriced bonds, overpriced stocks, and stocks in faraway places most investors
cannot spell will fall. Know the connections and understand
the risks. There is no substitute.

6. **Love experts, love their stock picks. They know what they
   are doing. They must be right.** No, they may be wrong.
   They are paid to be nice to the investment banking clients
   whose stocks they peddle, and they have their jobs because
   they promote trading. The track record of sell-side analysts
   is simply lamentable. The record of independent analysts is
   not quite so bad, but nothing worth following. A 2013 survey
   by the independent, Massachusetts-based research company
   CXO Advisory Group found that across all forecasts, accuracy was worse than the proverbial flip of a coin — just under
   47 percent. The best record was 68 percent, and the worst,
   22 percent. The average guru also had a forecasting accuracy
   of about 47 percent. The distribution of forecasting accuracy
   by the gurus looks very much like the proverbial bell curve —
   what you would expect from random outcomes. That makes
   it very difficult to tell if there is any insight to be had, much
   less paid for.

7. **Nirvana is at hand.** Hiring a new hand or firing an old one
   often leads investors to buy. A succession of new hands did
   not save Nortel, and it is arguable that very large companies,
   such as chartered banks or big life insurers, have so much
   momentum that nobody at the top is going to change much
   of anything. But, if there are reports that the chief financial
   officer was fired or last seen heading for Brazil, which seldom
   extradites, it could be a good moment to consider trading.
   Find out why there was a personnel change. And if it happens
   frequently, get out!

8. **Prosecution can't be ignored.** The U.S. Department of Justice
   has ruined many firms with excessively zealous prosecution.
   They destroyed accounting firm Arthur Andersen, though an

appellate court found it should not have happened. Still, you can't fight city hall. If the money is big and the opponent is a major government, especially the American federal government, consider getting out or wait until the fear is over and then consider getting in at a reduced price.

9. **Managing fate.** Coal companies' shares are cheap. Coal is dead. Some miners are bankrupt. Cheap alone is not enough of a reason to get in. Ditto industries being smashed by cheap imports. Get with the times. It is as wrong to go with old technologies as it is to be on new ones you do not understand. False correlations: of unrelated trends. Among the roster of spurious correlations is the near-perfect correlation of U.S. consumption of chicken and U.S. crude oil imports from 2000 to 2009. One correlation we like very much is deaths from venomous spiders in the U.S. to the number of letters in the winning word of the Scripps National Spelling Bee from 1999 to 2009.[8] Neither of these bizarre relationships has predictive value for the ups and downs to move in perfect synchronization. Nor has either relationship been tested for long-term persistence. For investors, the rule should be to study relationships, but don't bet on those that make no sense. Odds are they may work, but it is no way to make a living.

10. **The mirage of success through miscounting.** If you make an investment, the price doubles, and then you sell, the first half of the higher price is just return of your initial bet or capital. Your gain is 100 percent, not 200. This is an obvious point, yet many investors miss it.

11. **You can time the market.** No, you can't. Cheap can get cheaper and expensive even more so. Trade on fundamentals. Price is the last thing to consider. Everything else comes before. Where crime is a cover, it is foolish to speculate on the outcome. Sell if you are in, don't buy if you are not.[9]

12. **Fail to cope with regrets.** Loss is a fact, lament is an emotion. Use losses to sharpen your trading skills, and your loss will have generated a dividend of knowledge.

MATTERS OF TIMING

Some errors are benign. Investors often take the view that there is a good time to buy or sell. It seems true, but financial assets are not quite the same thing as a merchant's inventory of furniture or clothes or a grocers' cooler of lettuce. The difference is timing and inventory.

Stocks and bonds go on sale when other investors tire of them for reasons good or bad. The signs of fatigue, perhaps waiting for conditions to improve or the stock to rise, are dependent on the time of observation. Asset prices bounce, often like jumping beans, seemingly randomly — at least in the short run.

> Stocks and bonds go on sale when other investors tire of them for reasons good or bad. The signs of fatigue are dependent on the time of observation.

The investor can set a price for sale or purchase, but the question has to be whether the price will be a so-called limit order that acts as a trigger or the investor's own formula that a price is above or below a moving average. By using limit orders set on a stock's volatility, the investor avoids the mistake of trying to guess the exact moment when the stock is ripe for trading. The potential for error is still there, but it is moderated by the idea of using a price damper, the moving average, as a platform for the trading decision.

There is no substitute for vigilance. YBM Magnex, a Toronto-listed maker of bicycles and magnets — actually a front set up by Semion Mogilevich, a Russian-Ukranian mobster who specialized in large scale business crime — was a mid-cap market darling in the 1990s whose shares rose from a dime each to $20 before its frauds were exposed and it was delisted. It had good references. Former Ontario premier David Peterson was a director of the company, as was Owen Mitchell, a senior officer of a respected Canadian investment dealer.[10] With good credentials, it was an easy move to the Toronto Stock Exchange 300 Index in 1996, where YBM quickly became a favourite recommendation of analysts. But high-profile accounting firms declined to sign off on its financial statements. The lesson: When the concept — in this case bicycles and magnets — produces astronomical stock price valuations, go hunting somewhere else. And if you have an overpriced stock, take some money off the table or get out altogether.

Professional investment managers refused to believe that it was a criminal enterprise dressed up as a public company. Wise investors got out. Others waited for the market price to collapse and effectively force them out. The moral: Stocks wobble, but when stories of criminal activity surpass earnings estimates, it's time to go. Waiting only increases your chances of loss. A hefty dose of cynicism is a defence. And as a backstop, diversification is the final defence against major loss.

It comes down to deciding what is right, which stock to pick, when to sell a bond, and identifying what is simply dumb. One can minimize the cost of error by diligence. That means, among other things, understanding the market, understanding the asset, and having a sense of timing and what others are doing.

Stupid moves come in many forms, including failure to diversify, failure to keep fees under control, and failure to observe the broad economy or the economies of other markets in which one has invested. The more remote the market, the tougher it is to follow it. That is a reason to stick with what you know, what your experience provides as an advantage, and what your track record suggests is the right thing for you to do. Finally — and this is the end game for all investors — don't be the last person to leave the room when the proverbial music stops. Anticipation means staying alert to changes in others' actions. That may involve nothing more than reading newspapers or watching the news online. Sites like Bloomberg.com are free, precious tools for all investors.

BENOÎT POLIQUIN IN A MEA CULPA MOMENT

In 2005, I was thirty-one. I had worked as a portfolio manager for six years. My results were decent enough to be attracting new clients for my employer, a large securities firm. The market had been running up for about three years. Commodities were running up; the Chinese economy was firing on all cylinders and I felt I could do no wrong. I also felt like I should take risks. I also had purchased our first house, and my wife had interrupted her career to take care of our eighteen-month-old daughter. In retrospect, that was risk enough.

In short, I knew enough to be dangerous. I figured if I borrowed money from the equity of our family home and invested it, I could pay off the mortgage sooner. After all, if I could find the can't-lose opportunity, what could go wrong?

I wanted to find a company that had a high dividend, a solid balance sheet, and a business I could understand. Ideally, the company shares should be trading at a discount to what their intrinsic value was.

After a few months of research, I found what I was looking for and thought I could not lose. The stock was asset manager W.P. Stewart & Co Ltd. Stewart, the firm's head, had been a student of legendary value manager Benjamin Graham along with Warren Buffett. The firm had assets under management of US$2 billion. The firm paid solid dividends, had little debt, did good work, and marketed itself well. I bought in at $10 per share. It had a 7 percent dividend. I borrowed about $200,000 at 5 percent and got to keep 2 percent, which was a good return on my own equity in the deal, about half — net 4 percent. I had all of my own savings in the company's shares. It was a Warren Buffett stock. It had to work, I thought.

The stock shot up to $14 or so within a few months. I was so happy I told my wife. I wanted to sell, but she urged me to stay in. "Oh honey," I said, "the trend is our friend. This stock should trade for $20 if not $30 … so I will sell it then!"

But the stock started to fade … $13, $12 … then $10 again … in just a few months. How could I be so foolish? Well, selling now is just stupid … it will come back, I thought. So I doubled my efforts:

I researched further, called the company, and read every piece on the company I could find. The management included former Royal Navy officers — very blue blood indeed. I was convinced the stock would bounce back.

As it turned out, the firm's clients started to leave them, not because their portfolios or performance were lacking, but because newer ways to invest called hedge funds were all the rage. Hedge funds could borrow to increase their leverage and had fewer regulatory restrictions than conventional mutual funds. What's worse, key staff were also leaving the firm for the sexier offerings.

Stewart retired and new management arrived. The stock started to recover. I was sure I was in the right company in the right industry — my own.

But the asset under management kept falling, which led to lower sales and lower earnings. Dividends were reduced. Then ended altogether. My borrowing costs were no longer covered. I sold at $5 when the broker started calling to pay up the loan or put more money into the account. I decided to double down and increase my stake.

I borrowed from my credit cards to make the margin payments, paying nosebleed-percent interest in order to stay in a losing trade. It was utter foolishness — from a pro, no less. In retrospect, the rationale for accepting a loss is often too hard to face.

At $5, I had to sell. The broker was paid, but I was out $115,000. My wife was very upset.

Ironically, W.P. Stewart was sold in 2013 to a larger company, New York–based AllianceBernstein LP, with assets under management of US$447 billion.[12] I vowed to never invest so much on single bets and began the most difficult task of dissecting every part of this decision. Here is what I learned:

1. Never wager the nest. Borrowing against your home to invest is just plain stupid. It might make sense on a spreadsheet … until you have that position go against you.
2. Everything moves in cycles, and you want to be aggressive when everyone else is fearful and fearful when all are boastful. I went with the crowd. It was the wrong time to be aggressive.
3. Don't borrow to invest to the point where the bankers will force you to sell.
4. Dividends can and do get cut.
5. Don't invest in service businesses where the clients can leave at any time.
6. Management will be as honest as securities laws require, but that may not be honest enough.
7. You do not know as much as you think you do.

The lesson: Using leverage had me sweating as days turned into weeks and months. I could not wait to have the firm turn around and liberate me from debt. When you use leverage, you lose your own money fast … and the banks pull the loan when their money is at risk. The only protection is to structure your portfolio and your affairs in such a way that any mistake that will happen will not have a permanent impact on your financial life and those of your loved ones.

CONCLUSION

Trading Risk

Running any investment or investment portfolio is a venture into risk management. The names of the investments matter, for the risk and return profile of a web-based company with a lease, copyrights, and patents and a lot of very smart people is quite different from the risk profile of a real estate business with fortunes invested in concrete backed up by vast amounts of debt. But the risk/return relationship underlies every invest-ment and, for that matter, most ventures in life. To a cynic, investment is just trading risk, albeit in packages with company names. That's a healthy attitude, it should be said. Pity the investor who falls in love with a stock or bond or parcel of property. At the level of putting money into a business, love has no place.

The first and surely the most critical issue in evaluating a poten-tial investment and of monitoring investments one already has is risk evaluation. You have to ask if the game is worth the payoff. If not, you should go. If it is, then how much do you want to put on the line? These are not trivial questions. They are as appropriate for considering a purchase of a hundred shares of a bank as for tossing money into a junior gold mine. We mention those two examples, for Canadian and American banks are visible and reported on daily by the press while small cap gold mines may not be visible enough to attract the attention of the press or even of regulators. The point is, know who is on your side.

The perception of risk and the estimation of return are problems in psychology and behavioural finance. People familiar with a process or an industry, a game, or a quest may underestimate the risks. It is the conceit of insiders and it is inevitably dangerous. Likewise, the estimation of return, often from yesterday's stock market or a report of a recent, profitable sale of a house down the block, may make one think that the deal is repeatable. The fact that it is reported in the press is usually an indication that it is exceptional — in other words, an exception. But one oddity does not make a trend and one unusual case of profit or loss may be just that, an outlier. Know what matters and what does not. After all, the strongest force in investment markets is not continuation of trends, the notion that momentum persists, but the force of reversion to the mean, that whatever goes up will eventually come down and return to the average.

The momentum of stock prices or property prices from the average to the noteworthy to the spectacular — and then to the ridiculous — is a fact of life. Sometimes high prices stick, often because the underlying business is itself spectacular. More often than not — think back to the dot-coms — prices fall back to the level of others and often below. The wider the market and the more diversified the asset base, the less likely it is that the unusual will prevail. Thus, diversification of assets and time in the market are life preservers. The broader the investment and the more time it has to flower, the more likely the outcome will be profitable. The old saying, "It is time in the market, not timing the market," should not be forgotten. It is a golden rule.

Measuring the forces of momentum, which supports price trends, and mean reversion, which reverses them, is the investor's challenge. We don't think it can be done accurately for any one asset in isolation. But for a sector or a broad economy with identifiable metrics, it can work. It is all about the structure of the portfolio and the risks it bears. A portfolio is a composite of risks and returns or, put another way, what you can lose in comparison to what you can make. The loss part of the equation is embedded in debt that has to be serviced, perhaps inventory that has to be sold, perhaps pensions and future payments to employees, and suppliers who have to be paid. The gain is about potential sales, what customers will pay for what the portfolio's companies make and sell, profits to be realized, and the number of shareholders to whom the profits will be distributed, or, if not distributed, the earnings retained. Each of these variables breaks down into further components. The problem, of course, is to get a grip on what the profit less cost balance will leave for the shareholder.

It would be relatively easy to calculate sums and make suitable deductions for costs, but there is more. There is the effect of competition, taxation, regulation, and, these days, technological change. It is a huge analytical problem, but the idea of comparing what a giant retailer like Home Depot does to what a corner hardware store does is valid. Home Depot just does more of it.

> A portfolio is a composite of risks and returns or, put another way, what you can lose in comparison to what you can make.

The many risks of investing exist for all asset classes but in varying degrees. Liquidity is not much of an issue for stocks from large cap to small cap. Spreads between the bid and ask may widen a little, but trades for a few hundred shares are not hard to execute. For bonds, liquidity is not a problem for fresh government issues or large issues of familiar names like Royal Bank or Johnson & Johnson, but it is a huge issue for small issues of obscure companies that may not be rated by Moody's or Standard & Poor's or other services. Junk bonds as a whole are best left to specialty managers. They have the contacts and lists of counterparties to trade. Shift to developing markets, and debt and often stocks are harder yet to trade. Finally, in real estate, downtown properties in hot markets can be moved in a day, as can lots and houses in desirable suburbs. Invest in raw land in the hinterlands, scrub land in the north, or odd-shaped lots that are not good for much of anything and you can wind up a perpetual owner paying property taxes but unable to sell.

In this sense, liquidity and risk are almost synonymous. Often very high risk, which is really nothing more than the difficulty of trading quickly, goes with low-quality assets. And why not? If the asset is fine, many will want it and it will move quickly. In the end, liquidity reflects risk. It is not the whole story, but, normalized to honest businesses operating conventionally, it makes up a lot of the explanation of how to make and build your fortune.

We are coming to the idea and problem of testing the waters in any asset class. High liquidity means that a block of stock, say one hundred shares of the Bank of Nova Scotia, has low bid-ask spreads, and if you want to do the trade, it's done in an instant. Spreads between bid and ask, and thus trading risk, widen with uncertainty and complexity. Thus, real estate requires haggling and perhaps the hassle of what goes with a house, such as light fixtures and then legal fees and prepayment of some costs, reserves for others and so on.

Liquidity is measurable in stocks by looking at bid to ask price spreads. A couple of cents or a dime shows modest risk at the moment. Hard-to-trade small caps carry hefty speculative risk. When stocks can be optioned by puts and calls, which all large caps can, the trading risk is low and adept investors can lay off risk through options.

If your plan is to buy and hold an asset for a short time, the chances are the surprises in the form of new management, bad accounting, or earnings restatements that lower formerly reported profits won't happen. Of course, they still can, and if there is any doubt, see Nortel Networks. For the buy-and-hold investor with a horizon of five or more years, there is more that can go wrong, even though rising earnings and just simple inflation that drives up product prices will be on your side.

There is another dimension to risk, and that, as we have discussed, is diversification. Put all your money into one company's shares; one junk bond, which is often equity by another name; one real estate venture; and your chances of long-term success do not rise. Instead, if we use a risk to return equation, they diminish.

The cases of Solomon Huebner and Irving Fisher make the point. Fisher was an economist, perhaps the most famous of his day — the first three decades of the twentieth century. He created monetary economics and was famous, or infamous, for saying nine days before the crash of 1929, "Stocks are at a permanently high plateau." Then the New York Stock Exchange crashed, the Great Depression began, and Fisher began buying what he thought were cheap stocks. It did not work. Markets continued to fall to 1932. Fisher had piled his fortune into a few companies, and those shares shrivelled in value. He had to accept charity, living out his days in a house provided by Yale University.

In contrast, Huebner, the theorist of life insurance and risk management and professor at the Wharton School at the University of Pennsylvania, took the view that when stocks were cheap, it was not a time to plunge into a few bargain stocks. Rather, it was time to diversify. He said, "One share in fifty companies is better than fifty shares in one company because it gives the spread of averages." The outcome: Fisher died in poverty in 1947, while Huebner retired a rich man, until his own demise in 1964. The story, told in fascinating detail in Moshe Milevsky's wonderfully intriguing book, *The 7 Most Important Equations for Your Retirement*,[1] demonstrates the point that spreading risk not only adds to your chances for survival, but it also leads to longer sustained growth and wealth.

The concept of diversification has a counterweight, and that is depth of knowledge. People who work in the energy industry, for example, may through constant study of what they are doing and how conditions affect their businesses get an inside track on the affairs of the business. There are limits, of course, for discoveries of new oil reserves and important events for public companies have to be published. The downside of being an insider and thinking that a new gusher will change the world is that it may not.

In March 2008, oil was being sold at US$100 per barrel. No less an oracle than Goldman Sachs, the most influential bank on Wall Street, predicted that oil would hit US$200 per barrel in the not too distant future.[2] It didn't turn out that way, of course. Oil traded around US$65 a barrel in mid-2018. Tragically, investors who threw their life savings into the consensus and bet that oil prices were unstoppable lost their shirts, none more so than an Alberta midlevel oil executive afflicted with terminal cancer whose children were in danger of being taken to Russia by their mother, still a citizen of that nation, when her husband died. He knew the oil business and figured that the gains of upstream oil companies leveraged on what he thought would be the price of oil headed to the heavens would keep her in Canada. Dad died bankrupt with the fall of oil. Russia, famous for drafting young men into its brutal armed services training programs, probably got the kids. Single commodity bets, as his was, are perilous.

Diversification is not only insurance against misfortune, it is also an expression of modesty, for though one may think that, after many years of work in one industry or company, its affairs are understood, there is often more. The papermaking business, so robust in 1980 as newspapers and magazines gobbled up forests to be turned into pulp and then newsprint, was a catastrophe by 2015, with many plants closing for lack of sales. The internet wrecked the papermaking industry, something that probably few foresaw in 1990 when online publication was in its infancy. Today, with many publications having dropped paper publication entirely, you can buy paper mills for a promise to pay their debts and to clean up their ecology, perhaps to keep some employees working. It is not that the paper business cannot support profits, just that there is a lot less paper business to go around. Buying into the paper-making business cheaply has been a doubtful bet. Spreading your bets in the information industry, perhaps into Alphabet Inc., the new name for Google, as well as Facebook and the rest, has been far more profitable.

Hot stocks and hot sectors will continue to come and flourish and fade away. Our suggestions: Temper your insights by watching the market as you would your store. Experts at a distance are fine and may have useful insights. But just as you would not sell off most of your inventory to fill the store with one product, you should not narrow your portfolio or run on just one prediction that a single asset or even single asset class will win. It might. But the risk you take on is often higher than the potential gain from reducing diversification.

Just ask those who bet on video rentals. Remember Blockbuster, the video rental chain? It was a hot stock in the 1990s. At its peak in 2004, Blockbuster employed 84,000 people around the world. But video on demand and multinetwork choice systems on satellite television doomed the company. It filed for bankruptcy in 2010. Then on March 1, 2011, the U.S. Department of Justice filed a claim disclosing that Blockbuster did not have the funds to continue reorganizing and should liquidate. No matter how clever one might have been in the movie rental business, high download speeds doomed video rentals. Knowing a lot about late fees and three-for-one rental packages was, in the end, irrelevant.[3]

Investing is a moving target. Real estate, which is back in vogue as the hottest thing for money on the make, is a momentum play on what is happening in Toronto and Vancouver, in Paris with the return of financial exiles from London in the wake of Brexit, and in New York with the immense profits being rolled up in financial services. But no real estate boom is forever — just ask folks who lost their shirts in Spanish vacation properties in the 2008–2009 and later crash of European economies, Irish properties when the mortgage-lending-driven inflation of its banks went bust, and Japanese investors who thought the bubble of the 1980s had a solid foundation. It turned out that it did not.

> Hot stocks and hot sectors will continue to flourish and fade away, so temper your insights by watching the market as you would your store.

Those who bet on a trend inevitably bet on the recent past. The word "trend" itself expresses impermanence. There are no sure things, and surely none based on brief recent experience. The market for stocks and bonds, real estate, and, for that matter, such ephemera as baseball cards is never static.

We urge those reading *Cherished Fortune* to think not just in depth about the profits of a company, but in terms of where people are headed when they study, shop, spend, and retire. Just as a shopkeeper has to keep their finger on their neighbourhood, their customers, and competing shops that may sell what they sell or even other stuff that drains their customers' wallets, the investor in financial assets must follow what is happening to their money, their market, and the particular companies, funds, bonds, or whatever else he may own.

One can conceive of investing as a rarified pursuit of accounting and economics, but it is more understandable to view your fortune as a business you know intimately. It is not theories that matter in this view, it is what your stock — in both senses — is worth, what sorts of debts you may carry to run the business, and what your investment may earn in the future. And that, after all, is all it will ever be worth. The difference between cost to get into an asset and the profit or loss that rings the cash register when you leave is the rationale for investing. It is true for an investment portfolio manager shepherding hundreds of millions of dollars of stocks, and it is true for the small investor who runs their portfolio like a store whose business he knows well.

ACKNOWLEDGEMENTS

In assembling *Cherished Fortune*, we owe thanks to our mates, Vicki Laframboise and Heather Winters, without whose support *Cherished Fortune* would not have happened. We have to thank our editors at Dundurn Press, Kathryn Lane and Allison Hirst, as well as freelancer Jenny Govier, and editors Joe Hood and Pam Heaven at the *Financial Post*. We were assisted by investment experts at Exponent Investment Management, including Priyanka Ravindra, Graham Mayes, Mathew Hall, Stephan Desbiens, and Eliott Einarson, who deserve our appreciation, as well as friend and facilitator Deborah Steciuk. We have to thank our agent, Bev Slopen, computer expert Paul Jones, who rescued our digital lifeboat many times, researcher Daryl Kuhl, and bond authorities Chris Kresic and Edward Jong. We had advice from tax expert Don Forbes and financial planners Derek Moran, Graeme Egan, Caroline Nalbantoglu, and Dan Stronach, and counsel from Adrian Long, Brock Cordes, David Thompson, and Bryan Dunlop, who listened to our ideas as they moved from concept to manuscript to print. In spite of their guidance, any mistakes we have made are ours.

NOTES

INTRODUCTION

1. Friedman, winner of the 1976 Nobel Prize in Economics, was a critic of consensus, advocating among other things that the Federal Reserve Board set a permanent zero interest rate. For a discussion of his iconoclastic but valuable policy concepts, see Edward Nelson, "Friedman's Monetary Economics in Practice," Finance and Economics Discussion Series, Divisions of Research & Statistics and Monetary Affairs, Federal Reserve Board, April 13, 2011.
2. Peter Lynch, *One Up on Wall Street* (New York: Penguin, 1990).
3. Buttonwood Essay, *Economist*, March 5, 2016, 6.
4. Sidney Homer and Richard Sylla, *A History of Interest Rates*, 3rd ed. (New Brunswick, NJ: Rutgers University Press, 1996). See especially page 192.
5. Donald L. Roberts, "John Wycliffe and the Dawn of the Reformation," *Christianity Today* 3 (1983).
6. Michael Shermer, "How the Survivor Bias Distorts Reality," *Scientific American*, August 19, 2014.
7. Karen E. Klein, "How Survivorship Bias Tricks Entrepreneurs," *Bloomberg Business*, August 11, 2014.

CHAPTER 1: CROWDS

1. Jeremy J. Siegel, *Stocks for the Long Run*, 5th ed. (New York: McGraw-Hill, 2014), 6.
2. Giorgio Biscardini, Reid Morrison, David Branson, and Adrian del Maestro, "2017 Oil and Gas Trends," Strategy& (blog), PriceWaterhouseCoopers. strategyand.pwc.com/trend/2017-oil-and-gas-trends.
3. Susan Cain, *Quiet: The Power of Introverts in a World That Can't Stop Talking* (New York: Broadway Books, 2013), 88.
4. Cain, 90.
5. Brigit Katz, "Why Critics Are Skeptical About the Record Smashing da Vinci," Smithsonian.com, November 16, 2017. smithsonianmag.com/smart-news/da-vinci-painting-sells-record-breaking-450-million-180967246/.
6. Mark Landler, "Deutsche Bank Writes Down $3.1 Billion," *New York Times*, October 3, 2007.
7. George Parker and Patrick Jenkins, "Goodwin Stripped of Knighthood," *Financial Times*, February 1, 2012.
8. Wendy Stueck, "Bre-X Geologist Alive? His Widow Says Maybe," *Globe and Mail*, May 26, 2005. See also Steve Maich, "Bre-X Geologist Rumoured to Be Alive," *Maclean's*, June 7, 2006.
9. Quoted in Charles P. Kindleberger, *Manias, Panics, and Crashes: A History of Financial Crises*, 4th ed. (New York: John Wiley & Sons, 2000), 29.

CHAPTER 2: LEVERAGE

1. Sidney Homer and Richard Sylla, *A History of Interest Rates*, 3rd ed. (New Brunswick, NJ: Rutgers University Press, 1996).
2. Ben Protess, "U.S. Accuses Bank of America of a 'Brazen' Mortgage Fraud," *New York Times*, October 24, 2012.
3. Ruth Simon and Erik Brynildsen, "Who Benefits from Crowdfunding?" *Wall Street Journal*, March 30, 2016.
4. Tom Lauricella, "Market Hits 'Universal Life' Policies," *Wall Street Journal*, October 11, 2009.
5. John Caouette, Edward Altman, Paul Narayanan, and Robert Nimmo, *Managing Credit Risk: The Great Challenge for the Global Financial Markets*, 2nd ed. (New York: John Wiley & Sons, 2011), 117–26.

CHAPTER 3: VALUATION

1. Brian Hutchinson, *Fool's Gold: The Making of a Global Market Fraud* (Toronto: Knopf, 1998); Wendy Stueck, "Bre-X Geologist Alive? His Widow Says Maybe," *Globe and Mail*, May 26, 2005, updated March 28, 2017.

2. Sarah Hampson, "For Anne-Marie Sten, It's About Love — and Money," *Globe and Mail*, August 31, 2013. On the mines, see "Billionaire Khashoggi's Woes," United Press International, January 26, 1987.

3. Amy Feldman and Joan Caplin, "Is Jack Grubman the Worst Analyst Ever?" *Money*, April 25, 2002.

4. Rupert Neate, "Henry Blodget's Comeback Complete After $343m Sale of *Business Insider*," *Guardian*, September 29, 2015.

5. Abraham J. Briloff, *More Debits Than Credits: The Burnt Investor's Guide to Financial Statements* (New York: HarperCollins, 1976).

6. Goodwill is among the most intangible of assets. In an accounting sense, it is what one pays for stock or a business in excess of its stock market price. It sometimes backfires. On July 26, 2001, a tech company, JDS Uniphase, announced it would write down US$44.8 billion of the value of companies for which it had overpaid. It was, at the time, the largest goodwill write-down in history. The write-down accompanied the dismissal of sixteen thousand workers in its various plants, nine thousand before the announcement and seven thousand more after. See Barnaby J. Feder, "JDS Uniphase Will Write Down $44.8 Billion in Assets," *New York Times*, July 27, 2001.

7. Aswath Damodaran, *Investment Valuation: Tools and Techniques for Determining the Value of Any Asset* (New York: John Wiley & Sons, 2002). See also Damodaran, *Investment Philosophies: Successful Strategies and the Investors Who Made Them Work* (New York: John Wiley & Sons, 2003).

8. Benjamin Graham and David L. Dodd, *Security Analysis* (New York: McGraw-Hill, 1934).

9. Briloff, *More Debits Than Credits*.

10. Avner Mandelman, *The Sleuth Investor* (New York: McGraw-Hill, 2007).

11. Jeremy J. Siegel, *Stocks for the Long Run*, 5th ed. (New York: McGraw-Hill, 2014), 96.

12. Carol J. Loomis and Joel Keehn, "The Biggest, Looniest Deal Ever," *Fortune*, June 18, 1990.

13. Nassim Nicholas Taleb, *The Black Swan: The Impact of the Highly Improbable* (New York: Random House, 2007). See also Michael T. Burr, "Black Swans and Turkeys," *Fortnightly Magazine*, November 2010.

CHAPTER 4: BONDS

1. Carmen M. Reinhart and Kenneth S. Rogoff, *This Time Is Different: Eight Centuries of Financial Folly* (Princeton, NJ: Princeton University Press, 2009), 23, table 2.1.

2. Jeremy J. Siegel, *Stocks for the Long Run*, 5th ed. (New York: McGraw-Hill: 2014), 6.

3. Siegel, 6.

4. Siegel, 96.

5. "The Grotesque Campeau Failure," *New York Times*, January 17, 1990.

6. See "Advisory: Non-Viability Contingent Capital," Office of the Superintend of Financial Institutions Canada, August 2011. osfi-bsif. gc.ca/Eng/Docs/nvcc.pdf.

CHAPTER 5: STOCKS

1. Brooke Sutherland, "Here Comes GE's Turnaround Plan: It Better Be Good," *Bloomberg Business Week*, October 27, 2017.

2. The Mawer New Canada Fund, with 57 companies in its portfolio, turned in an average annual compound gain of 12.0 percent for the ten years ended March 31, 2018, compared to its benchmark's 3.6 percent average annual compound return in the same period.

3. For data showing the non-persistence of leadership by managed funds, see "Mutual Fund Performance Persistence," CXO Advisory Group, June 21, 2012. cxoadvisory.com/21090/investing-expertise/mutual-fund.

4. Abraham J. Briloff, *More Debits Than Credits* (New York: Harper & Row, 1976).

5. James P. O'Shaughnessy, *What Works on Wall Street: A Guide to the Best-Performing Investment Strategies of All Time* (New York: McGraw-Hill, 1998).

6. Harry Domash, *Fire Your Stock Analyst* (New York: Prentice Hall, 2003). See valuation standards on pages 28 to 40.
7. Aswath Damodaran, *Investment Fables* (New York: Prentice Hall, 2004), 96–100.
8. O'Shaughnessy, *What Works on Wall Street*.
9. See "Guru Grades," CXO Advisory Group Gurus. cxoadvisory.com/gurus.

CHAPTER 6: REAL ESTATE

1. Richard S. Newman, *Love Canal: A Toxic History from Colonial Times to the Present* (New York: Oxford University Press, 2016).
2. See Douglas Martin, "William Zeckendorf Jr., 84, Dies; Developer Put Stamp on Skyline," *New York Times*, February 13, 2014.
3. *Economist*, October 7, 2017, 24.
4. "Bankruptcy," *Economist*, October 7, 2017, 75. See also Daniel Fisher, "Detroit Tops the 2012 List of America's Most Dangerous Cities," *Forbes*, October 18, 2012.
5. Robin Finn, "The Killer Assessment: NY Condo Gets Hit with $30 Million Assessment," *New York Times*, June 12, 2014.
6. Douglas Gray, *Making Money in Real Estate*, rev. ed. (Toronto: John Wiley & Sons, 2005), 254–56.
7. Gray, 62.

CHAPTER 7: MISTAKES

1. Didier Sornette, *Why Stock Markets Crash: Critical Events in Complex Financial Systems* (Princeton, NJ: Princeton University Press, 2003).
2. Sornette, 61–63.
3. Nicholas Nassin Taleb, *The Black Swan: The Impact of the Highly Improbable* (New York: Random House, 2007).
4. Jeremy Siegel, *Stocks for the Long Run*, 5th ed. (New York: McGraw-Hill, 2014).
5. Larry Berman, "Glued to the Rear View Mirror," *Globe and Mail*, September 12, 2016, B5.
6. The Minsky Moment is a subset of credit cycle theory. See Justin Lahart, "In Time of Tumult, Obscure Economist Gains Currency

— Mr. Minsky Long Argued Markets Were Crisis Prone: His 'Moment' Has Arrived," *Wall Street Journal*, May 12, 2008.

7. See recent Dow member changes: Matt Jarazemsky and Colin Barr, "Alcoa, H-P and Bank of America to Be Dropped from the Dow Jones; Goldman Sachs, Nike and Visa to Be Added to Benchmark Index," *Wall Street Journal*, September 11, 2013.

8. Tyler Vigen, Spurious Correlations. tylervigen.com/spuriouscorrelations.

9. Jeff Gray, "After 17 Years, Bre-X Case Finally Closes," *Globe and Mail*, April 23, 2014.

10. "YBM Magnex Used by Mob to Bilk Investors," CBC News, June 8, 1999.

11. "AllianceBernstein L.P. Completes Purchase of W.P. Stewart & Co., Ltd.," PR Newswire December 12, 2013. prnewswire.com/news-releases/alliancebernstein-lp-completes-purchase-of-wp-stewart--co-ltd-235639331.html.

CONCLUSION

1. Moshe A. Milevsky, *The 7 Most Important Equations for Your Retirement* (Toronto: Wiley, 2012), 149.

2. Louise Story, "An Oracle of Oil Predicts $200-a-Barrel Crude," *New York Times*, May 21, 2008.

3. Christopher Harress, "The Sad End of Blockbuster Video: The Onetime $5 Billion Company Is Being Liquidated as Competition from Online Giants Netflix and Hulu Prove All Too Much for the Iconic Brand," *International Business Times*, December 5, 2013.

FOR FURTHER READING

BONDS

Allentuck, Andrew. *Bonds for Canadians: How to Build Wealth and Lower Risk in Your Portfolio.* Toronto: Wiley, 2006. A primer on investing in government and corporate bonds.

Crescenzi, Anthony. *The Strategic Bond Investor: Strategies and Tools to Unlock the Power of the Bond Market*, 2nd ed. New York: McGraw-Hill, 2010. A sophisticated examination of the bond market and trading methods.

Thau, Annette. *The Bond Book*, 3rd ed. New York: McGraw-Hill, 2011. A lucid discussion of bond mechanics with U.S. emphasis.

STOCKS

Bogle, John C. *The Little Book of Common Sense Investing: The Only Way to Guarantee Your Fair Share of Stock Market Returns.* New York: Wiley, 2007. The rationale for use of exchange traded funds from a U.S. perspective by the theorist of index investing.

Damodaran, Aswath. *Investment Fables: Exposing the Myths of Can't Miss Investment Strategies.* Upper Saddle River, NJ: Pearson, 2004. Investment concepts measured for success. Vital reading for the serious investor.

Eichengreen, Barry. *Hall of Mirrors: The Great Depression, the Great Recession, and the Uses — and Misuses — of History*. New York: Oxford University Press, 2015. It's all here — the subprime boom, Bernie Madoff, Lehman Brothers ... by one of the best macroeconomists in the world. Read it and laugh and weep.

Ilmanen, Anti. *Expected Returns: An Investor's Guide to Harvesting Market Rewards*. New York: Wiley, 2011. A fund manager explains portfolio theory.

Ineichen, Alexander M. *Absolute Returns: The Risk and Opportunities of Hedge Fund Investing*. New York: Wiley, 2002. The author calibrates returns to various theories.

Lo, Andrew W. *Adaptive Markets: Financial Evolution at the Speed of Thought*. Princeton, NJ: Princeton University Press, 2017. A broad review of investment concepts based on portfolio theory and behavioural economics. Fascinating and very readable.

Malkiel, Burton G. *A Random Walk Down Wall Street: The Time-Tested Strategy for Successful Investing*. New York: W.W. Norton, 2015. Defence of index investing by a distinguished American academic. The foundation of the idea that managers with fees almost never beat indices over the long run.

Milevsky, Moshe A. *The 7 Most Important Equations for Your Retirement: The Fascinating People and Ideas Behind Planning Your Retirement Income*. Toronto: Wiley, 2012. Far more than a retirement book, this small tome reviews the foundations of long-term income generation and consumption in complex math made very understandable.

Mulford, Charles W., and Eugene E. Comiskey. *The Financial Numbers Game: Detecting Creating Accounting Practices*. New York: Wiley, 2002. All about earnings management, reporting fictitious revenue and other accounting sins. Essential reading for the serious investor.

O'Shaughnessy, James M. *What Works on Wall Street: A Guide to the Best-Performing Strategies of All Time*, 4th ed. New York: McGraw-Hill, 2012. Demonstrates the merits of using price to sales as a predictor of returns.

Reinhart, Carmen M., and Kenneth S. Rogoff. *This Time Is Different: Eight Centuries of Financial Folly*. Princeton, NJ: Princeton University Press, 2009. A compendium of bond defaults organized historically and written with subtle humour. If you think of buying foreign bonds, read this first.

Schilit, Howard. *Financial Shenanigans: How to Detect Accounting Gimmicks & Fraud in Financial Reports*, 4th ed. New York: McGraw-Hill, 2018. Title says it all. Very readable.

Siegel, Jeremy J. *Stocks for the Long Run: The Definitive Guide to Financial Market Returns and Long-Term Investment Strategies*, 5th ed. New York: McGraw-Hill, 2014. Compares asset class returns for two centuries. Vital perspective in a readable form.

Singal, Vijay. *Beyond the Random Walk: A Guide to Stock Market Anomalies and Low-Risk Investing*. New York: Oxford University Press, 2004. A lucid discussion on how to profit from stock market anomalies.

Sornette, Didier. *Why Stock Markets Crash: Critical Events in Complex Financial Systems.* Princeton, NJ: Princeton University Press, 2003. Before 2008, this math-y but understandable book by a geophysicist predicted the cataclysm, though not the date, with a promise of more to come. Read it and grit your teeth.

PROPERTY

Gray, Douglas. *Making Money in Real Estate*, rev. ed. Toronto: Wiley, 2012.

OTHER SOURCES

The Successful Investor. Weekly tips on stocks distilled into dividend investing, Canadian shares, American shares. Available by subscription from The Successful Investor, 218 Sheppard Ave. E., Toronto, ON, M29 3A9; 416-756-0888.

The daily press, including the *Financial Post* and the *Globe and Mail*'s *Report on Business* are valuable sources of current and retrospective investment information. The *Wall Street Journal* and *Barron's* are valuable sources of U.S. and global information and insight.

INDEX

ABOUT THE AUTHORS

ANDREW ALLENTUCK is a columnist for the *Financial Post* and the author of textbooks on economics and consumer problems, problems of investing, the economics of retirement and retirement planning, and bond investing, as well as many hundreds of articles on asset management. Andrew is the author of *Bonds for Canadians* (Wiley), *When Can I Retire?* (Penguin), *Who Speaks for the Patient?* (Burns & MacEachern), and *The Cost of Age* (Fitzhenry & Whiteside), and the co-author *of Consumer Choice: The Economics of Personal Living* (Harcourt Brace Jovanovich).

BENOIT POLIQUIN is president and lead portfolio manager at Exponent Investment Management in Ottawa, and is a chartered financial analyst and a certified financial planner. Benoit is also advisor to the Family Finance series in the *Financial Post*.

Book Credits

Acquisitions Editor: Scott Fraser
Project Editors: Kathryn Lane and Jenny McWha
Editor: Jenny Govier
Proofreader: Dawn Hunter
Indexer: Elena Gwynne

Cover Designer: Laura Boyle
Interior Designer: Courtney Horner

Publicists: Michelle Melski and Tabassum Siddiqui

Dundurn

Publisher: J. Kirk Howard
Vice-President: Carl A. Brand
Editorial Director: Kathryn Lane
Artistic Director: Laura Boyle
Production Manager: Rudi Garcia
Director of Sales and Marketing: Synora Van Drine
Publicity Manager: Michelle Melski

Editorial: Allison Hirst, Dominic Farrell, Jenny McWha, Rachel Spence, Elena Radic
Marketing and Publicity: Kendra Martin, Kathryn Bassett, Elham Ali, Tabassum Siddiqui, Heather McLeo

 dundurn.com   dundurnpress
 @dundurnpress   dundurnpress
 dundurnpress   info@dundurn.com

FIND US ON NETGALLEY & GOODREADS TOO!

DUNDURN